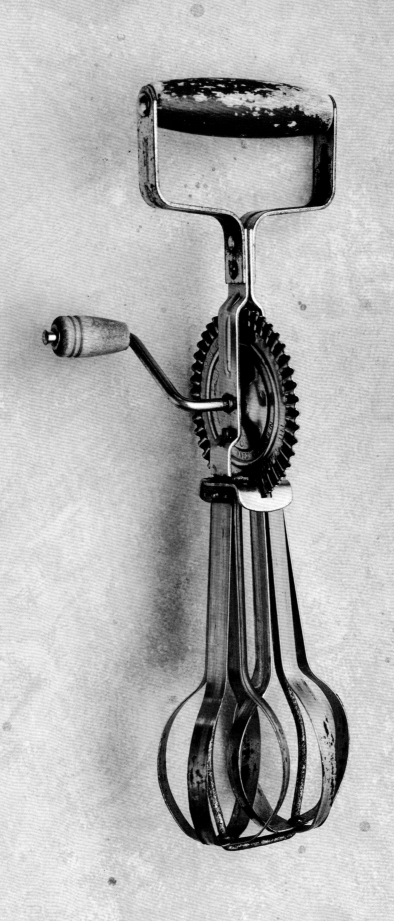

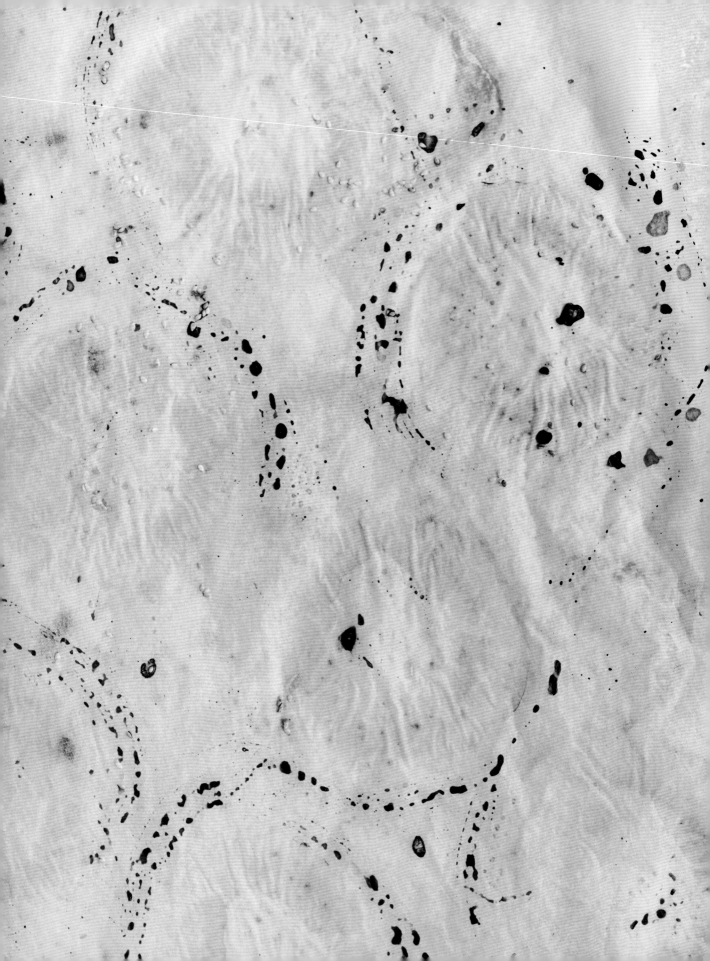

Crust

Essential Sweets and Savories from Victoria's Beloved Bakery

Tom Moore

WITH REBECCA WELLMAN

appetite
by RANDOM HOUSE

Appetite by Random House® and colophon are registered
trademarks of Penguin Random House LLC.

Library and Archives Canada Cataloguing in Publication
is available upon request.

ISBN: 978-0-525-61238-4
eBook ISBN: 978-0-525-61239-1

Book design: Jennifer Griffiths
Typesetting: Daniella Zanchetta
Book photography: Peter Bagi and Rebecca Wellman
Photo on page xiii by Dominic Hall

Printed in China

Published in Canada by Appetite by Random House®,
a division of Penguin Random House Canada Limited.
www.penguinrandomhouse.ca

10 9 8 7 6 5 4 3 2 1

appetite
by RANDOM HOUSE | Penguin
Random House
Canada

This book is for my biggest fans—my kids.
Abby and Sam, watching your love of cooking
grow as you do fills my heart with joy.
Olivia and Zac, I'm so grateful that we are
a part of each other's lives. I couldn't love the
four of you more.

"I need some sugar in my bowl, I ain't foolin';
I want some sugar in my bowl."

NINA SIMONE

Contents

This Is Me

My culinary career began at an early age, many years before Crust Bakery was even a glimmer in my eye. I have endless memories of being in the kitchen with my mum and both of my grandmothers, music on in the background, helping them cook and bake. At the time, I thought I was very helpful, though in reality, I am sure I was only licking the mixer paddle and getting in the way. (I'm sure my Crust staff will tell you that this is sometimes still the case!) These early experiences shaped and defined me in ways for which I am forever grateful.

I grew up in Tamworth, in rural Australia, where my parents ran a culinary and medicinal herb farm called the Moore Creek Herb Farm. My dad was a pharmacist, my mum an artist. We had chickens and cows, vast gardens, trees, and shrubs full of fruit and berries—but we were terrible farmers, as my mum and dad were city slickers by nature. However, we loved our animals and basked happily in our farm life. Our yard was vast, and we were surrounded by gardens full of produce and herbs, the delicate scents and flavors infusing us with their earthly inspiration and embedding themselves in our pores and psyches. All four of us kids have a deep love of food and cooking, with our parents inspiring, encouraging, and teaching us about growing produce, applying science and creativity in the kitchen, and generally appreciating all the good things in life. At our home, we often hosted friends and family for celebrations, my parents sometimes leaving us kids fully in charge of the menu! We would fill the table with platters and plates stacked high with breads and meats, fresh vegetables and salads, cakes,

cookies, and pies, the food always the centerpiece of such occasions, guests exclaiming with surprise and delight at what we had come up with. It was an idyllic childhood, waking to the scent of fresh baking on the weekends, music always playing throughout our house, plenty of room to run and play in our 110-acre yard, and growing up enveloped by a supportive, loving family. With these surroundings and my pure love of all things culinary, I was destined to pursue a career in cookery.

Fast-forward to 1992: I was halfway through grade 11, effortlessly achieving straight A's and completely bored. I felt so over my stodgy, patronizing teachers and their lessons, which I found useless, given my deep chef-like passions and arrow-straight ambitions. What did I need geography and history for when all I wanted was to cook? (Though I must admit, math and science did come in handy for my future baker self.) I expressed my dissatisfaction to my parents, and to my utter surprise, they told me that if I was so sick of school and didn't want to go, then I didn't have to—but I *did* have to study. Within the month they had me enrolled at a local trade school in a six-month course on small-business catering. This was an exhilarating change, and I was eager to get started with my new life! I was the youngest in the class, as you can imagine, and I nailed it! It's easy to excel when you are living what you love. The instructor told me that if I wanted to be a chef, I needed to get out of Tamworth and apprentice at a top hotel or restaurant in the big city of Canberra (pronounced *Can-Brah*, in true Australian fashion). Taking his advice, I immediately enrolled in an esteemed culinary school, and started my apprenticeship at the huge, bustling five-star hotel, Capital Parkroyal. I was so young, and very nervous to be leaving my comfortable and familiar home and neighborhood. But I knew what I wanted, and I was ready.

Parkroyal taught me the skills of classic French cooking, the art of fine pâtisserie (which proved to serve me more than I knew at that time), and how to work in a kitchen with dozens of others, the heat and steam, and the click-clack of knives as we cooked and baked for hundreds and hundreds across the hotel's massive restaurants and ballrooms. Three years later, by the age of nineteen, I had won the title of Australian Apprentice Chef of the Year by the Australian Vocational Education and Training Authority. I was spent and satiated, and after years of early mornings, killer-long days, and intense learning, I needed a rest and a change.

"Bite off more than you can chew, then chew like hell!"

So, after a few more years working around Australia, I landed a job as an executive chef in the city of Victoria on Canada's west coast, a ferry ride away from Vancouver. I saw it as a great learning opportunity to manage a large kitchen staff, something that would be very useful in the restaurant and bakery kitchens of my future. But I was still very young and worried that my youth would cost me some of the respect that typically comes with age. So I grew a goatee and told everyone that I was ten years older than I really was. It seemed to work! I learned a ton about leading a kitchen, and I made some lifelong mates—I was particularly taken with Crystal, the front-of-house manager, who shared my love for food, travel, and restaurant culture. Two years after we met, we married and moved back to Australia with entrepreneurial hearts and big ambitions. Back in Canberra, Crystal and I decided to open a restaurant together. We called it Sage, in honor of my herb farm upbringing, and it felt, in a way, like I was bringing a little piece of my childhood home to my new life. It comforted me in its familiarity, even if only in name.

The next few years were exciting and extremely gratifying. Sage was a hidden gem in the heart of Canberra: an intimate fine-dining restaurant focused on local, modern Australian cuisine. We won numerous accolades, including a prestigious Chef's Hat and a consistent standing as one of the top ten restaurants in Canberra, as determined by the *Sydney Morning Herald*. I started to be recognized in a community of like-minded people. I was regularly asked to contribute food-related articles and recipes to the local newspaper, and often appeared as a guest chef at events around town and at several private cooking schools. This environment fed my soul, and I felt an immediate kinship with anyone who showed an interest in cookery and baking, learning of my love for teaching, writing, and engaging with them. It was a very happy time.

My mantra has always been "Bite off more than you can chew, then chew like hell!" This proved to be poignant, as around the same time that I was diving into Canberra's culinary community, some dear friends who were exhausted and overwhelmed by the industry offered us their restaurant, called Grazing, and I also began lecturing, training apprentice chefs, and judging cooking competitions at the Canberra Institute of Technology. I loved carrying on Grazing's emphasis on quality regional ingredients—including produce from the restaurant's own half acre of vegetable patches and herb gardens, fifty chickens, and two beautiful orchards, all of which my kitchen team and I would lovingly tend—and solidifying my passion for teaching and guiding young chefs at the institute. But with two restaurants and a lecturing job, something had to give! So, after several years, we sold Sage, and I left the institute. Then shortly thereafter, chewing like hell, I opened my own chef apprentice school, called ForChefs. This allowed me to focus on my teaching and Grazing.

Crystal and I had started a family by this point, and it was a joyous but admittedly messy few years. As much as I loved being in the kitchen at Grazing, I began to realize that the chef life might not be suited to the schedule and goings-on of my young family. My daughter, Abby, was four now, and my son, Sam, just a baby. Long hours and late nights had kept me away from my kids, and I was not okay with that. Grazing and ForChefs were both in good shape, practically running themselves, and while I knew I needed to make yet another change, I was not willing to leave the industry entirely. Weighing my options, I decided to start a pâtisserie, aptly named Knead. I felt my new endeavor would be a practical next move: unlike the grind of late-night restaurant service, I would be up in the wee hours instead, before my kids were even awake, and home early enough to play and take part in their daily routines. It proved to be a good fit and a real turning point for me, taking me in a more family-friendly direction. Despite being bleary-eyed and a little rumpled, I was awarded the title of Australian Young Restaurateur of the Year by Appetite for Excellence, and I was happily embedded in the culture of food and teaching, baking, running a restaurant, raising children, and living a good life.

Sadly, right around that time, Crystal's father passed away unexpectedly, so we decided to go back to Crystal's hometown of Victoria, British Columbia, to be with family. Returning to Canada was something we'd always planned on, but these sad circumstances pushed our timeline ahead. It was difficult to leave Canberra, of course, but I knew I needed a change and a rest, so we pulled up our roots, sold the businesses, and headed back to Victoria. Once we arrived, we took a few months off to concentrate on family and settle into our new home and neighborhood. Predictably, I began to get restless. In keeping with a family-friendly work schedule and my love of baking, I started researching spots for a new bakery—opening a bakery in Victoria had always been part of our vision. I knew where I wanted it to be: in the food district of downtown's Fort Street. So I started knocking on doors and making inquiries, and eventually came across a lovely space that had, for at least the last fifty years, been some iteration of a bakery. It felt like fate.

Crust became an immediate success. We had learned a lot from our previous ventures, and we wanted to bring something to our bakery that was reflective of that: customer-focused, homemade, unpretentious, crave-worthy food. We kept our offerings simple but unique (with flavors like lemon and passion fruit, frangipane, and lots of chocolate), our menu consistent in quality, and our service impeccable. Crust is a homestyle bakery—reflective of us—rustic sweets and savories on display in our big street-facing window, coffee and sandwiches on freshly baked bread for our lunchtime guests, and custom cakes and desserts to order. Before long, lineups started weaving down the street before our doors opened in the morning, and local critics, writers, and "best in the city" contests awarded us accolades. Even though I was no longer living in my beloved Australia, I felt like I was home again.

Although Crystal and I went our separate ways in our marriage by the end of 2015, we remain business partners to this day. She takes care of the front-of-house operations, and I bake, teach, and manage the staff in the kitchen. We have a good thing going, and with Crust now well established, a new kiosk at Uptown mall in Victoria, and my kids in high school, growing fast and finding more independence, something that had been in the back of my mind for years began to pop up regularly in my thoughts and dreams: I wanted to write a cookbook, to send a little bit of Crust to the kitchens of our visitors who want to bring our treats home to friends and family, even if they don't live in Victoria, and even to share with folks who had never waited in our morning queues. I wanted to take all the experience of a commercial bakery and modify it for a home kitchen in a beautiful visual memento of our humble shop, full of photos, recipes, tips, tricks, and techniques. I enlisted the help and experience of my friend Rebecca Wellman, a food writer, stylist, and photographer, who already had a few books under her belt, and we were on our way.

Within these pages, you will find a combination of recipes we offer at Crust and ones I make at home. Yes, baking is technical, and measurements need to be accurate, but it doesn't have to be fussy, complicated, or intimidating. Through all the restaurants I've owned, the classes I've taught, and the people I've met, what has always felt true is that food is love. That feeling of connecting over food, and the appreciation of the bounty we are so fortunate to enjoy, is what I am delighted to share with you here.

Today, some of my favorite times are spent in my home kitchen with my kids, my wife, Pennye, and her two teenagers. It is a full house, just like the one I grew up in, with plenty of music, laughter, and epic kitchen dance parties. And when I go home to Australia to visit, we plan our entire trip around food. We spend three days with the whole family—kids and cousins, aunts and uncles—all cooking together and trading secrets in a delightful whirlwind of catching up and reveling in one another's presence, to soak up all we can during our too-short visit. This is what food means to me. Family and love and gathering and togetherness. And I am delighted to share that with you. These days, I continue to bite off more than I can chew, but I must admit, I am finding great satisfaction in chewing a little more slowly.

Tom

How to Get the Most out of a Baking Book

First and foremost, before you start on any baking projects, I highly encourage you to read this entire book—like a novel. I might be joking a little, but really, you will get so much out of reading all my tips and guidelines, the recipes themselves, and the kitchen notes accompanying many of the recipes.

Check out the Equipment (page 7) and Ingredients (page 11) sections to best know how to stock your supply cupboards (which tools do you *really* need, and which ones can you skip?) and your pantry (spoiler: good quality is always preferred, but what *makes* a product good quality?).

The Baking Fundamentals chapter (page 15) is like a mini master class, taking all the experience of a commercial bakery and modifying it to fit your home kitchen. For example, what is blind-baking? Why do we sift flour? And how many times have you read "don't overmix!"—what does it actually mean? Baking Fundamentals is where you'll find all the answers.

Then on to the recipes! We wanted to fill this book with all kinds, some that are a bit on the easier side and others that offer more of a challenge for those who enjoy that sort of thing. This is a book of essentials: muffins, cookies, brûlées, cheesecakes, breads, and other basics that are wonderful to have in your repertoire, ready to whip up at any time. We often hear that baking is a science, and that measurements must be exact and precise to prevent horrible disasters. But I believe baking doesn't need to be stuffy and uptight. While it is important to measure and weigh as accurately as you

can, don't get too fussed about it. Feel free to play and experiment. Go into baking with an open heart and a relaxed attitude. We learn the best things when we play.

Finally, it's great to know what can go wrong and how to fix it. The Troubleshooting guide on page 255 can help you anticipate and avoid common mishaps before you've wasted those dozen egg whites or the carefully sourced passion fruit. But if you find yourself running into trouble while baking, check the guide, learn from your mistakes, and try again!

I genuinely hope that everything you bake turns out magnificently, but there is no way I can account for the variables that exist in my kitchen versus yours, including the altitude, humidity, and temperature where you live, your oven and baking vessels, the brand of products you use, and, of course, your personal taste. Be sure to experiment to see what works best for you.

I want this to be your journey, and I am excited to introduce you to all the Crust recipes in this book. Make them your own. Have fun, take pride, and please, no matter what happens, be sure to eat it anyway!

Equipment

We all have a baking wish list, don't we? While there is room for adaptation in baking vessels and tools, this list provides an example of the ultimate collection that makes baking life easier, less stressful, and ultimately convenient. Pick and choose as you wish or aim to have them all—provided you have the cupboard space!

ANGEL FOOD CAKE PAN/TUBE PAN: These are the traditional shape for angel food cake. You want a straight-edged pan with a removable center to allow you to take the cake out easily.

BAKING PANS WITH REMOVABLE BOTTOMS: A wonderful addition for the home baker who has everything, these are lovely for easily popping a whole square or cake out of the pan.

BENCH SCRAPER/PASTRY SCRAPER: A scraper makes picking up dough off a flat surface much easier and helps prevent breaking and cracking. It's also useful for cleaning up dough scraps that are stuck to the counter.

BLOWTORCH/CRÈME BRÛLÉE TORCH: When my mum made lemon meringue pie, she would put the whole pie, raw meringue on top, in the oven to brown. This is an option, of course, but a torch allows for more precision and artistry. Also, if you like to make brûlées, a torch is a must.

BUNDT CAKE PAN: This pan makes for a beautiful presentation and helps thicker batters bake more evenly, without overbaking and drying out on top.

COOKIE SCOOPS: If you are an avid cookie baker, scoops are perfect for providing the same size cookies every time. I use them to scoop out muffin and cupcake dough as well! Either a 1- or 2-ounce (30 or 60 g) scoop will do nicely, but I've included my preference within each recipe.

FOOD PROCESSOR: This is great for mixing some of the doughs in this book and is a nice-to-have appliance for chopping and blending nuts, herbs, and other ingredients.

HAND MIXER: This mixer is perfect for when the job doesn't warrant hauling out the stand mixer. It's great for whipping cream, batters, and eggs.

IMMERSION BLENDER: Sometimes combining ingredients requires full emulsification: mixing two ingredients together that typically don't mix well, such as oil and water. Although a brisk whisking by hand can work, an immersion blender is the most effective way to emulsify. It will make all the difference to the rise and fluffiness of your baked goods.

MICROWAVE OVEN: I would never bake or cook anything in the microwave, but when small amounts of butter or chocolate need softening or melting, it's a fine option. Always be sure to use a glass or ceramic vessel that is both food- and microwave-safe.

OFFSET SPATULA: These are especially helpful for spreading frosting or smoothing out the top of batter that is already in the pan. Offset spatulas typically come in small or large sizes—choose which is best based on the size of your pan or baked good and what feels best in your hand. A palette knife also does the trick.

PARCHMENT PAPER OR MAT: Because of its nonstick, ovenproof quality, we use parchment paper a lot at Crust to line sheet pans and to transfer items from one place to another. Pro tip: scrunch up the paper before smoothing it out onto a sheet pan or fitting it into a baking vessel. That way, it won't roll back up on itself and will be easier to handle. Silicone or baking mats are another excellent option for lining sheet pans; the biggest restriction of mats is that they only lie flat and cannot be used in a round tin or a deep bowl.

PASTRY BRUSH: For egg washes or greasing pans, brushes made of silicone, synthetic, or natural hair all work well. For fine work, I use an artist's natural-hair paintbrush.

PASTRY CUTTER: With a row of thin metal strips or wires attached to a handle, a pastry cutter is used to incorporate fats, like butter or lard, into dry ingredients, like flour. While you can also use your hands, a pastry cutter allows you to complete the task without warming up the fat with the heat of your hands.

PIE WEIGHTS: Small clay orbs that are used for blind-baking pie crust, pie weights alleviate the need to poke holes in the bottom of your pastry shell. They're the better option if you're pouring liquid into the crust, to prevent leaking.

PIPING BAGS AND TIPS: You can apply frosting with an offset spatula, a knife, or the back of a spoon for most of these recipes, but if you'd like to get a little fancy, piping bags and tips are nice to have. Specific shapes and sizes are suggested in the recipes, but feel free to be creative! There are many interesting options to choose from at kitchen specialty stores. For starters, a 12 mm round tip and a 10 mm star tip will do the trick.

ROLLING PINS: These come in two main styles: standard (a thick cylinder with handles at each end) and French (one solid piece, tapered at each end). Standard can be easier on the hands if you are doing a lot of rolling, but

the moving parts mean it is more vulnerable to breaking. In the end, it comes down to ergonomics. Whatever type of rolling pin you prefer, be sure to get one long enough to roll out a decent-size piece of dough, such as for an 11-inch (28 cm) pie crust. Pins also come in different materials, such as marble, wood, or plastic. If you are partial to a wooden one, be sure to wash it right after use and don't let it sit in water for too long.

SCALE: If there is one must-have in your kitchen, it's a scale. Weighing ingredients is far more accurate than measuring by volume, giving a precise and consistent measurement every time.

SHEET PANS: It's nice to have a mixture of large and small sheet pans, some with rims, some without. I suggest keeping a 13 × 18-inch (33 × 46 cm) pan (also known as a half sheet) and a 9 × 13-inch (23 × 33 cm) pan (also known as a quarter sheet).

SIEVES/STRAINERS: A fine-mesh sieve is perfect for sifting dry ingredients, straining batters and mixes, and draining berries or other wet ingredients. Even better, keep a few on hand with different gauges of mesh. For example, it's nice to have a superfine mesh for dusting with cocoa powder or icing sugar.

SKEWERS/CAKE TESTERS: You can certainly get "proper" cake testing skewers, which are often made of metal, but toothpicks and wooden shish kebab skewers work just as well.

SPOONS AND SPATULAS: A few good wooden spoons, sturdy spatulas, and large metal spoons are great for spooning, scraping, and stirring. Both wood and silicone will pick up scents and flavors, so don't leave your spoons sitting in a pot of curry or anything pungent. (You could even label your spoons as "sweet" and "savory.") For wooden spoons in particular, make sure to wash and dry them right away, as they won't be happy spending too much time sitting in soapy water.

SPRAY BOTTLE: It is great to have two of these: one bottle with water, for spritzing bread when baking it; and another small one with oil, for greasing cake tins and pans.

SPRINGFORM PANS: Springforms are necessary for cheesecakes and other delicate cakes. They come in many different sizes. If you only have room for one, a 9-inch (23 cm) pan is perfect.

STAND MIXER: Often, a stand mixer is the most practical and efficient tool for mixing ingredients. Not all baking recipes require a stand mixer, but the recipes in this book that call for one do! It might be tricky to obtain the required texture without the power of an electric motor. If you don't have one, an electric hand mixer, a whisk, a wooden spoon, or, in some cases, your hands might work well—I never want to discourage you from trying a recipe! However, if you are a serious baker, I do recommend investing in a stand mixer.

TART TINS AND RINGS: Tart tins and rings vary in size and depth. Tart rings are round stainless steel rings that have no bottom; they are placed on a parchment-lined sheet pan, then the pastry is tucked up the sides to create the shell. You can also get tart tins with removable bottoms, sometimes with scalloped edges; the pastry is draped inside along the bottom and sides, then, once baked, is removed by pushing the bottom of the pan upward to release the shell. Finally, there is the multi-tart tin, which is similar to a muffin pan. All of these tart tins will work for the recipes in this book. Depending on the pan's size, you may have excess dough or filling, and you may need to adjust the baking time slightly. Large tart tins can also come with removable bottoms and in several different materials, such as ceramic, aluminum, or glass. If you don't have a large tart tin, a pie plate will do.

THERMOMETER: Here's another important tool: a good-quality, ovenproof, digital instant-read thermometer is essential for checking doneness in breads, measuring the temperature of oil for deep-frying, and even checking the accuracy of your oven.

WHISKS: A standard wire whisk is a must for blending ingredients effectively. For thick doughs or batters, or anytime you don't want to incorporate too much air, use a Danish dough whisk, which is flat with a curlicue in the center of the wire circle.

WIRE COOLING RACK: It's good to have one or two shapes and sizes of racks for cakes, cookies, muffins, and large loaves.

Ingredients

I cannot stress enough the difference that good-quality ingredients will make to your baked goods. We're all familiar with the odd craving for strawberries in the middle of winter, and sometimes that freezer stash will do just fine, but other times it pays to eat seasonally, shop locally, or even grow your own! When it comes to organizing my pantry, I might be obsessed. Tidy, uniform containers full of flours, sugars, chocolate chips, and other shelf-stable, top-quality ingredients are some of my favorite things. Of course, the list of possible ingredients is rather endless, but here are a few tips when it comes to the most commonly used ones.

ALMOND FLOUR: Make sure your almond flour (also known as almond meal in Australia) is a quality product, made of pure almonds, and that you keep it fresh. Store it in an airtight container in a cool pantry for up to 2 months, in the fridge for up to 4 months, or in the freezer for up to 6 months. Because almonds contain oil, the flour can go rancid; let your nose be your guide.

BUTTER: Quality unsalted butter all the way! Butters from grocery stores vary greatly, and the choices can be overwhelming. Consider things like color: some butters are more yellow than others, which isn't ideal for a white icing, for example. (To avoid this, look for beta-carotene on the label, which makes butter more yellow; however, color also depends on the cow's diet.) For purity of taste, look for butter that has only cream in the ingredients list. You won't find me using salted butter in my baking, as unsalted allows me to control the salt content in the

recipe. However, if salted is all you have, go ahead, just decrease the amount of salt in the recipe. When the recipe states "at room temperature," leave butter on the counter for 1–3 hours, depending on the amount and the temperature in your kitchen. It should be soft. When the recipe says "cold," it means straight from the fridge. Unsalted butter can be kept on the counter for 2–3 days, but is susceptible to going rancid, so you be the judge. Otherwise, it will keep in the fridge for as long as the manufacturer specifies.

CHOCOLATE: I can't stress enough how important it is to go for quality chocolate. Whether it's chips, chunks, or bars, strive to find pure chocolate with no fillers for that genuine, rich, deep chocolate flavor. Do some research and taste-testing, especially when chocolate is the star player in a recipe, such as the Chocolate Peanut Butter Tart on page 33 or the Chocolate, Bourbon, and Pecan Butter Tarts on page 47. Well wrapped, pure chocolate will keep at room temperature or in the freezer for up to 6 months.

CITRUS JUICE: Always, always squeeze fresh juice from your citrus fruits! The dull, metallic taste of bottled juice is just not the same, and if you use bottled citrus juice, your finished dish will definitely be compromised. Keep citrus in the fridge until ready to use and roll it firmly on the counter before squeezing to get the juices flowing!

COCOA POWDER: As with chocolate, quality is key here. Look for Dutch-processed dark cocoa powder, not the generic lighter brown powder. Dutch is less bitter than standard cocoa because of how it is processed, so it's much more suitable for many baked goods. As far as brand, I recommend Valrhona. It will make a world of difference. Cocoa powder will keep in a cool, dry place for 6 months. After that, it may begin to lose its flavor potency, but it will not be unsafe to consume.

CREAM: Be careful with the whipping cream brand you use. Find cream that has no gums; some contain a stabilizer, such as guar gum, which works great for whipping, but not for baking, as it can change the texture of the baked good. Expiration dates are included on cream cartons, of course, but use your senses to determine if it's still usable.

CREAM CHEESE: Look for Philadelphia-style cream cheese without fillers such as gums. Gums, while generally harmless to most people, do not like heat; they may curdle and not stay stable. The Philadelphia brand is reliable. Cream cheese should be kept in the fridge until its expiry date. If you need to soften it, do so by leaving it out on the counter for about 1 hour before use.

EGGS: All the eggs in this book are large, or about 1.8 oz (50 g) each. If the recipe says "cold," they need to be *cold*, right out of the fridge. If the recipe says "at room temperature," leave them on the counter for about 1 hour before use. Do not leave eggs out for more than 2 hours. If you forget to take them out of the fridge in time, place them in warm water for about 10 minutes to warm them a bit, then use right away. If the recipe does not specify the temperature of the eggs, it doesn't matter! Unwashed eggs fresh from the farm that haven't been refrigerated yet can be kept on the counter for about 2 weeks. Otherwise, keep them in the fridge and note the expiration date.

FLOUR: This is a very important ingredient, and as there is so much on offer out there, including garden-variety grocery store flour, locally milled flour, and all sorts in between, it is worth knowing a few things. With all flours, always go with unbleached, store in a cool, dark place, and don't eat it raw. Buy it in small amounts, as it can go rancid. Be sure to check the expiration date on the package.

▸ **ALL-PURPOSE FLOUR** works very well in many recipes, and I do recommend organic.

▸ **BREAD FLOUR**, although it's not essential, is definitely ideal for baking bread, as the gluten in bread flour is higher than in all-purpose, meaning your dough will have more structure and rise, and the bread will have a bouncier, chewier crumb. The bread recipes in this book all call for bread flour, and I generally mean a reputable, good-quality, unbleached white bread flour, minimally processed, with as few additives as possible. Small-batch flours are great, but so are Bob's Red Mill or King Arthur. If you use all-purpose for bread, it will still turn out fine, but it might take longer to mix and develop the needed gluten, so you may need to experiment with the timing of kneading and proofing.

▸ **CAKE FLOUR AND PASTRY FLOUR** can be used interchangeably, and either is a huge benefit when making cakes and pastries. These flours have less gluten protein than all-purpose, so the dough or batter will develop less stretch and the baked product will be lighter, which is what you want in a cake or pie.

▸ **GLUTEN-FREE FLOUR** should be used only if it's a reputable, high-quality kind (like King Arthur and Bob's Red Mill). Be sure to read the label to ensure the flour can be substituted 1:1 for all-purpose. I would not recommend substituting gluten-free flour in the bread recipes in this book, as they are developed and written specifically for glutinous flour.

▸ **WHOLE WHEAT, RYE, AND OTHER FLOURS** are lovely. If you decide to sub one in for all-purpose flour in the recipes in this book, I say go for it! Just know that the recipe may need to be adjusted. Experiment and discover what you enjoy!

FRUIT AND HERBS: Organic, seasonal, and fresh is always best. Full stop. Although grocery store fruit and herbs are perfectly acceptable, I do recommend farmers' markets or, if I may be so cheeky, homegrown! Yes, growing your own fruit may be a bit challenging, but an herb garden is a wonderful and simple addition to any yard, patio, or balcony. Buy or harvest your herbs in small batches and keep them in a glass of water in the fridge, covered with a plastic bag, for optimum freshness.

OIL: A good-quality, neutral, organic vegetable oil such as canola, sunflower, or safflower is great for greasing baking tins and for use in baking. Organic extra virgin olive oil is best for finishing and drizzling. Purchase all oil in small amounts, and keep it well sealed in a cool, dark place. Look for opaque bottles, which prevent degradation from light, and before using oil in your baking, give it a sniff to ensure it isn't rancid.

SALT: This important ingredient can vary by brand and style. Depending on the size of the grain or flake, it can measure by volume differently, so it's a good idea to be consistent and get to know your salt. Kosher salt is a workhorse and is great for adding and enhancing flavor. It is pure, with no fillers, and is consistent in its saltiness. Table salt is an acceptable substitute if that is all you have, but I prefer the purity of kosher. Sea salt quality differs depending on its source and where in the world it comes from. Flaky sea salt is excellent for finishing and adding a salty factor to your something sweet—a favorite combination of mine! Salt in its pure form has no expiration date, so long as it's kept dry.

SUGAR: Keep sugar in a cool, dry place. Technically, sugar will not spoil, but its taste may be compromised if not used within a couple of years.

▸ **GRANULATED SUGAR** is the most common one to have on hand, and can be processed at home to do the job of either superfine sugar or icing sugar.

▸ **SUPERFINE SUGAR** is used when the sugar needs to dissolve fast. You can make your own by grinding granulated sugar in a food processor or blender for 1–2 minutes or until the granules become finer, while maintaining some of their grittiness.

▸ **ICING SUGAR** is used for finishing and to make frosting and icing. You can make your own by grinding granulated sugar in a food processor or blender for 6–8 minutes or until there is no more grittiness. Be sure to use it right away; otherwise, it may start to stick together. Measure the sugar required *after* grinding it.

VANILLA: While all of these types of vanilla essentially come from the same source, there are subtle differences that shine through when baking with each of them. The type you use really comes down to personal preference, whether it be for flavor, appearance, or convenience.

▸ **VANILLA EXTRACT** should be pure. It will keep indefinitely in the pantry because of its alcohol content. Avoid vanilla essence or synthetic flavoring.

▸ **VANILLA BEAN PASTE** is an excellent alternative and can be used 1:1 in place of extract. It is nice to use when you want visible flecks of vanilla seeds in your baked good. Look for an expiry date on the jar.

▸ **VANILLA BEANS** are great if you don't have extract or if you want to showcase the vanilla flecks in your final product. The seeds scraped from about 2 inches (5 cm) of a fresh vanilla bean are equal to about 1 teaspoon of extract. Don't waste your money putting beans in cakes or anywhere they will get lost in the dish. Beans will maintain optimum flavor for about a year in a cool, dry place.

Baking Fundamentals

Baking takes practice. There is a bit of a science to the way yeast forms, how flour reacts to water, and how caramel comes together with sugar and heat. While there is definitely room for creativity after you have some experience under your belt, a methodical approach to baking is a good way to start. Instinct will begin to kick in once you've made a recipe a few times, especially when it comes to more technical goods like bread and pastry. Below you will find some time-tested tricks and tips that will give you a leg up on all your baking adventures.

1. **WEIGH YOUR INGREDIENTS:** You've heard it before, and I will say it again: weigh your ingredients. There is nothing more significant when it comes to accuracy and consistency in baking.

2. **PREP YOUR OVEN:** Ovens vary greatly between manufacturers, and one oven's 350°F (180°C) may be another's 360°F (182°C). A thermometer is a great way to measure your oven's accuracy and, more importantly, to learn whether it tends toward hot or is on the cooler side. When preheating, even if your oven buzzes to tell you it's ready, leave it for another 15 minutes. Unless otherwise specified in a recipe, set the oven rack in the center. Don't forget that the oven will cool when you open it to put the food in, so be quick and keep that in mind when timing your dish. If you have a fan-forced or convection oven, you may need to lower the heat a touch from what's listed in the recipe.

3. **PREPARE YOUR BAKING VESSELS:** Throughout the recipes, you will often see the familiar phrase "Spray or brush the pan with a neutral oil and line it with parchment paper." Why and how do we do this? Lightly brushing or spraying a tin with a quality, fresh, neutral oil (such as canola oil) will help keep your baked goods from sticking to the pan. It will also help to create a thin browned layer on the bottom of the treat, encouraging flavor and helping to prevent it from breaking or cracking. Paper is another layer of insurance against sticking, and often provides an aid to pull a loaf or cake out of its pan. In a rectangular or square pan, two crisscrossed pieces of parchment—one lengthwise, one widthwise, each overhanging the edges by about an inch (2.5 cm)—is effective. For a round pan, cut a round of parchment the same size as the bottom of the pan.

4. **SOFTEN YOUR BUTTER:** Where specified, it's important to use room-temperature butter. If your room is on the cold side, heat the butter very gently, without melting it, which would make for a different consistency entirely when the butter is added to other ingredients. Softening butter makes it much easier to blend evenly, and when you beat it together with sugar, the mixture will form air bubbles, which expand when baking. It is very difficult to beat a cold stick of butter.

5. **SIFT YOUR DRY INGREDIENTS:** You may think sifting flour and other dry ingredients is a needless step, but when sifting is called for, it's for good reason. Sifting flour

removes any clumps, making it easier to blend evenly with other ingredients. In most cases in this book, the flour and other dry ingredients are measured before sifting. If you have a sifter, go ahead and use that; otherwise, shaking the ingredient through a fine-mesh sieve works well.

6. **TOAST YOUR NUTS, SEEDS, AND SPICES:** Unless otherwise specified, be sure to toast these ingredients, as toasting brings out their deep, earthy flavors and makes a world of difference to your finished dish. Nuts and larger seeds benefit from being toasted on a sheet pan in the oven at a moderate temperature. Smaller seeds and spices can be toasted in a dry cast-iron skillet on the stove. Nuts and seeds are full of fats, so keep them moving by giving the sheet pan or skillet a shake or a stir, and keep your eye on them—they will burn quickly. Nuts and seeds get crunchier as they cool, so use the color (a light toasty brown) as your guide to when they're done, not the texture.

7. **SAVE YOUR EGGS FROM THEMSELVES:** It would be a huge bummer to have a bowl full of beautiful batter, break an egg into it, and see a bit of shell spin away as it gets sucked into the bowl by the whisk attachment. Crack eggs into a small bowl before adding them to your other ingredients.

8. **AVOID OVERMIXING:** How many times have you read this and asked yourself what exactly it means? It's important to combine ingredients so they are blended just enough to make a uniform dough or batter, keeping the mixture aerated to create a fluffy, moist crumb. More mixing means more gluten formation—not always something you want. Overmixing can cause a tough and sometimes gummy result. Fold or gently stir ingredients together just until you no longer see any dry pockets of flour, then stop mixing and go on to the next step.

9. **DON'T SKIP THE BLIND BAKE:** "Blind-baking" means to bake a pastry crust in advance of adding the filling. If you were to add a jug of eggs and cream to a raw pastry shell, the crust would never bake! Before blind-baking, line the top of the pastry with a round piece of parchment paper and weigh it down with pie weights or dry beans to keep it from puffing up and baking full of bubbles. You can poke the pastry all over with a fork instead, but holes might remain in the bottom of the crust—not great if you're adding soupy fillings. You would also need to keep a close eye on the pastry as it bakes, because it may puff up despite its many holes.

10. **REST YOUR DOUGH:** Resting allows flour to properly absorb liquid, making it easy to handle and to ensure it's evenly mixed. In the case of bread, a rest gives gluten time to form and flavor a chance to develop. For baked goods that require a rest, it is an important step, so don't skip it or rush it.

11. **USE YOUR SENSES:** While I can state the time it takes to complete a recipe step, ultimately the best way to judge that something is ready is by the way it smells, looks, and feels. This takes practice, so follow the cues in the recipes and learn to recognize the sensory signs of readiness.

12. **PRESERVE PROPERLY:** Whether you are keeping a baked good on the counter, in the pantry, or in the fridge or freezer, take the time to wrap it properly so it's airtight. Make sure it has cooled completely before wrapping. Use good-quality freezer storage bags or containers, and mark the expiry date on the package. (You might think you'll remember—you won't.) When freezing individual goods, like cookies, freeze them for 2–3 hours on a sheet pan, then transfer them to a freezer bag or container. That way, they won't stick together.

Pies and Tarts

"This is Monday and I'm making pies;
I'm making pies. Making pies."

PATTY GRIFFIN

Lemon Passion Fruit Slice

2 cups (250 g) graham cracker crumbs

⅓ cup (80 g) unsalted butter, melted

1-2 Tbsp (15-30 ml) hot water (100-110°F/38-43°C)

6 egg yolks (keep the whites for the Swiss meringue!)

2 cups (500 ml) sweetened condensed milk

1 tsp finely grated lemon zest

1 cup (250 ml) fresh lemon juice

½ cup (125 ml) fresh or thawed frozen passion fruit juice (see note)

1 recipe Swiss Meringue (page 241; see note on page 39)

1 cup (125 g) assorted berries, such as blueberries, blackberries, and raspberries

I have wonderful memories of wandering out to the backyard as a kid, feet bare, sun bright, and picking a warm, ripe passion fruit off the vine that grew up our back fence. My siblings and I would cut the fruit in half and suck out the seedy, sour flesh, while the juice ran down our chins and onto our toes. Years later, I worked for my dear friend and baker Lee Primmer, who ran the Gods Café in Canberra, where Lee served a fantastic lemon slice. Lee continues to inspire my baking to this day, as this recipe shows, and the passion fruit twist honors my childhood memory and adds a lovely perfume, tartness, and tropical note to the dessert.

1. Preheat the oven to 350°F (180°C). Spray or brush a 9-inch (23 cm) springform pan with a neutral oil and line the bottom with parchment paper.

2. In a medium bowl, combine the graham crumbs, butter, and 1 tablespoon (15 ml) of the hot water. Mix with a wooden spoon until combined. It should clump together when you squeeze it between your fingers. If it doesn't, add a bit more hot water.

3. Transfer the graham mixture to the prepared springform pan and press down with your fingertips until flat and even. Smooth out using the back of a large spoon, then cover and place in the fridge until ready to use.

4. In a large mixing bowl, whisk together the egg yolks and condensed milk (see note). Whisk in the lemon zest, lemon juice, and passion fruit juice until well combined.

5. Pour the mixture immediately onto the graham crumb base and spread gently with a spatula. Place the springform pan on a parchment-lined rimmed sheet pan.

6. Bake until the passion fruit mixture is set and the center doesn't jiggle, 15–20 minutes. Let cool to room temperature.

7. Cover loosely with plastic wrap and refrigerate for at least 1 hour, until chilled, or ideally overnight.

8. Make the Swiss meringue just before you are ready to serve.

9. If moisture has formed on top of the slice, dab the top with a clean paper towel, removing as much moisture as possible. Pipe the Swiss meringue on top of the cake, using a 12 mm round piping tip (or your favorite tip!). You can torch the top lightly using a small blowtorch, but the slice will be just as good without. Decorate the top with the berries and serve immediately.

This cake will keep in an airtight container in the fridge for up to 3 days. I don't recommend freezing the finished cake.

KITCHEN NOTES:

1. Don't let the yolks touch the sweetened condensed milk until you are ready to mix them together; otherwise, the sugar in the condensed milk will affect the yolks, and you will have bits of cooked egg yolks through the cake.

2. If you are using fresh passion fruits, strain out half of the seeds and discard them. If you are purchasing the passion fruit juice, make sure it's pure. I would avoid canned juice or pulp. Real, fresh passion fruit juice should be very tart and floral-tasting, with no sugar added. You can often get this juice frozen from specialty food shops or online. If passion fruit juice is too hard to find, pure raspberry juice makes a fine substitute.

3. Cut this cake using a wet knife, warmed in hot water and rinsed well in between cuts.

Vanilla Crème Brûlée Tarts

½ cup (100 g) granulated sugar, plus more for torching

1 tsp all-purpose flour

¼ tsp kosher salt

4 egg yolks, lightly whisked

2 cups (500 ml) whipping cream

2 tsp pure vanilla extract

1 tsp vanilla bean paste (see note)

½ recipe Sweet Pastry (page 236), cold

The creamy crackling of crème brûlée in a convenient little tart! To make crème brûlée "to go," I figured what better vessel than pastry? Buttery crust, sensual and melty, creamy vanilla filling, and the satisfying crack of brûlée sugar come together beautifully. This is a signature Crust dessert that we are well known for; we make more of these than any other tart. It is a classic combination that customers love to take home and present to family or guests as a simple but impressive dinner party dessert.

1. In a large mixing bowl, whisk together the sugar, flour, and salt. Whisk in the egg yolks until well combined. Carefully whisk in the whipping cream in two additions, then the vanilla extract and paste. Don't whisk too hard or fast—you don't want to overmix and aerate the cream or you'll end up with little soufflé tarts, which can collapse and be difficult to torch.

2. Strain the mixture through a fine-mesh sieve into a large measuring jug or bowl. Cover with plastic wrap and let rest in the fridge for at least 1 hour, and preferably overnight.

3. Spray or brush eight 4-inch (10 cm) tart rings with a neutral oil and place them on a large parchment-lined sheet pan.

4. Remove the pastry from the fridge and let it sit at room temperature for about 10 minutes.

5. On a lightly floured surface, using a floured rolling pin, gently roll out the pastry to an even thickness of about ⅛ inch (3 mm). (Rolling it out between two sheets of parchment paper makes life easier.)

6. Using a cookie cutter or a thin-rimmed glass, cut out eight 5-inch (13 cm) circles. Line each tart ring with the pastry, pressing it in well around the edges and bottom. Avoid leaving any air pockets between the pastry and the rings, and make sure there are no cracks where the brûlée mixture can leak out. (If needed, gently combine the pastry scraps, without overworking, then wrap and refrigerate for 30 minutes before rerolling and cutting. Discard any leftover pastry after rolling it the second time.)

7. Using a small knife, trim the excess pastry from above the sides of the tart rings so that the pastry is flush with the ring. Cover the rings with plastic wrap and refrigerate for 30 minutes.

8. Meanwhile, preheat the oven to 350°F (180°C), with a rack on the bottom rung.

9. Gently stir the brûlée filling, then pour it slowly into each tart ring. Fill the pastry right to the top or it will be challenging to torch later.

continued →

10. Bake for 25–30 minutes, rotating the pan a half turn after 12 minutes, until the pastry is golden brown and the filling has risen slightly and is firm when you gently wobble the pan. Let cool to room temperature for at least 30 minutes.

11. Carefully remove the tarts from the rings and place them one at a time on a large metal tray turned upside down (see note), ready to torch. Be careful not to turn the tarts upside down, as the filling is delicate.

12. Working with one tart at a time, lightly and evenly sprinkle it with some sugar—you only need a light coating to start. The secret to a good brûlée is all in how evenly you apply the sugar. Using a small blowtorch, gently wave the flame over the sugar until it begins to melt. Try not to get much color on the sugar at this point, and torch inward to avoid burning the pastry.

13. Sprinkle a second layer of sugar evenly on the top of the tart. Be very careful, as the molten sugar is very hot and will give you a terrible burn if it gets on your skin! Gently wave the blowtorch over the sugar again, evenly melting the sugar. You will start to see some color form as the sugar caramelizes.

14. Repeat a third and final time and torch until the sugar turns a light caramel color. Be careful not to over-torch the sugar, as burnt sugar tastes bitter and terrible.

15. Repeat steps 12–14 with the remaining tarts. This can be a tricky process and might take some practice.

16. Let the molten sugar cool slightly, then carefully use a spatula to transfer the tarts to a wire rack to cool completely, about 15 minutes.

These tarts are best eaten within 1 or 2 hours of torching; otherwise, the sugar starts to soften. If made ahead, prior to adding the sugar, they will keep in an airtight container in the fridge for 1–2 days; however, this will soften the pastry. Best to be on the safe side and eat them right away.

KITCHEN NOTES:

1. If you don't have vanilla bean paste, feel free to leave it out—no need to replace it with more extract. Since vanilla is the star of this recipe, it's just nice to have the seeds from the paste flecked throughout the custard.

2. When torching, I place the tarts on the back of a large, clean sheet pan so the heat from the torch isn't transferred to my countertop.

Triple Chocolate
Crème Brûlée Tarts

½ cup (90 g) semisweet
dark chocolate chips

2 Tbsp (16 g) cocoa powder,
sifted

1 tsp instant coffee
granules

2 cups (500 ml) whipping
cream

1 tsp pure vanilla extract

½ cup (100 g) granulated
sugar, plus more for
torching

1 tsp all-purpose flour

¼ tsp kosher salt

4 egg yolks, lightly
whisked

1 recipe Chocolate Pastry
(page 236), cold

When I was an apprentice chef, we had a chocolate tempering machine that automated the process of heating and cooling, heating and cooling. I used to imagine lying underneath this machine with my mouth open, allowing the chocolate to drizzle directly into my mouth, such was my obsession. And while my Willy Wonka–like fascination has always existed, it wasn't until much later in my career that I understood the value of really good chocolate. I've learned about the origin and the methods used to create the best-tasting, smoothest, creamiest chocolate, and now I strive to use only premium chocolate in my baking. My appreciation continues to grow as I refine my knowledge, because once you've tasted great chocolate, you simply cannot go back. This chocolate-on-chocolate-on-chocolate dessert is made for the passionate aficionado, so be sure to seek out the very-best-quality chocolate you can find.

1. In a heatproof bowl, combine the chocolate chips, cocoa, and coffee granules.

2. In a medium pot, warm the cream over medium-high heat. Stirring slowly, bring the cream to a boil.

3. Just before the cream comes to a rolling boil, pour it over the chocolate chips. Stir until the chocolate is completely melted and thoroughly incorporated. Add the vanilla extract. Do not stir too quickly; you don't want to aerate the mixture. Let cool, uncovered, for at least 20 minutes.

4. In a large mixing bowl, whisk together the sugar, flour, and salt. Whisk in the egg yolks until well combined. Carefully whisk in the chocolate cream mixture in two additions. Don't whisk too hard or fast—you don't want to overmix and aerate the cream or you'll end up with little soufflé tarts, which can collapse and be difficult to torch.

5. Strain the mixture through a fine-mesh sieve into a large measuring jug or bowl. Cover with plastic wrap and let rest in the fridge for at least 1 hour, and preferably overnight.

6. Spray or brush eight 4-inch (10 cm) tart rings with a neutral oil and place them on a large parchment-lined sheet pan.

7. Remove the pastry from the fridge and let it sit at room temperature for about 10 minutes.

8. Lightly dust a work surface and a rolling pin with a bit of cocoa or flour. Gently roll out the pastry to an even thickness of about ⅛ inch (3 mm). (Rolling it out between two sheets of parchment paper makes life easier.)

continued →

9. Using a cookie cutter or a thin-rimmed glass, cut out eight 5-inch (13 cm) circles. Line each tart ring with the pastry, pressing it in well around the edges and bottom. Avoid leaving any air pockets between the pastry and the rings, and make sure there are no cracks where the brûlée filling can leak out. (If needed, gently combine the pastry scraps without overworking, then wrap and refrigerate for 30 minutes before rerolling and cutting. Discard any leftover pastry after rolling it the second time.)

10. Using a small knife, trim the excess pastry from above the sides of the tart rings so that the pastry is flush with the ring. Cover the rings with plastic wrap and refrigerate for 30 minutes.

11. Meanwhile, preheat the oven to 350°F (180°C), with a rack on the bottom rung.

12. Gently stir the brûlée filling, then pour it slowly into each tart ring. Fill the pastry right to the top or it will be challenging to torch later.

13. Bake for 25–30 minutes, rotating the pan a half turn after 12 minutes, until the pastry is golden brown and the filling has risen slightly and is firm when you gently wobble the pan. Let cool to room temperature for at least 30 minutes.

14. Carefully remove the tarts from the rings and place them one at a time on a large metal tray turned upside down (see note on page 24), ready to torch. Be careful not to turn the tarts upside down, as the filling is delicate.

15. Working with one tart at a time, lightly and evenly sprinkle it with some sugar—you only need a light coating to start. The secret to a good brûlée is all in how evenly you apply the sugar. Using a small blowtorch, gently wave the flame over the sugar until it begins to melt. Try not to get much color on the sugar at this point, and torch inward to avoid burning the pastry.

16. Sprinkle a second layer of sugar evenly on the top of the tart. Be very careful, as the molten sugar is very hot and will give you a terrible burn if it gets on your skin! Gently wave the blowtorch over the sugar again, evenly melting the sugar. You will start to see some color form as the sugar caramelizes.

17. Repeat a third and final time and torch until the sugar turns a light caramel color. Be careful not to over-torch the sugar, as burnt sugar tastes bitter and terrible.

18. Repeat steps 15–17 with the remaining tarts. This can be a tricky process and might take some practice.

19. Let the molten sugar cool slightly, then carefully use a spatula to transfer the tarts to a wire rack to cool completely, about 15 minutes.

These tarts are best eaten within 1 or 2 hours of torching; otherwise, the sugar starts to soften. If made ahead, prior to adding the sugar, they will keep in an airtight container in the fridge for 1–2 days; however, this will soften the pastry. Best to be on the safe side and eat them right away.

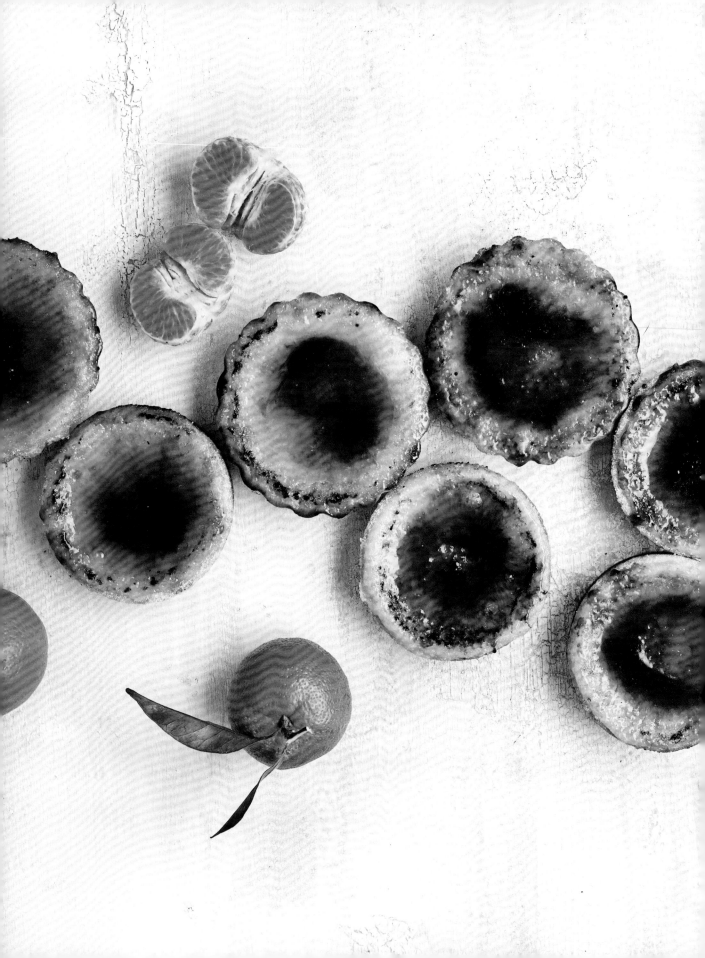

Mandarin Crème Brûlée Tarts

Mandarin Purée

3 small mandarins

Brûlée Tarts

½ cup (100 g) granulated sugar, plus more for torching

1 tsp all-purpose flour

¼ tsp kosher salt

4 egg yolks, lightly whisked

2 cups (500 ml) whipping cream

1 tsp pure vanilla extract

1 recipe Sweet Pastry (page 236), cold

In Canada, kids often find a mandarin orange tucked into the toe of their Christmas stocking. We did not do this in Australia, as we didn't even have stockings! It took me a while to get used to the concept of stockings PLUS presents under the tree, but once I had embraced the idea, Crystal and I decided to honor Canadian tradition and started doing this for our kids too. We quickly learned that kids don't typically choose oranges over chocolate and candy canes, and so I wanted to find a use for the rogue mandarins that were left behind. Although many orange recipes have a hint of zest or orange water or essence, this recipe takes it one step further. I wanted these tarts to pack a punch and to highlight the mandarin, which complements the cream and crusty torched sugar top. Boiling and puréeing mandarin peels brings out the floral intensity of the fruit and takes these directly to the next level.

———————

1. **MAKE THE PURÉE:** Peel the mandarins and place the peels in a small saucepan. Set the fruit aside for another use. Add water until the peels are completely covered and place a tight-fitting lid on the pot. Bring to a boil, then turn down to a simmer and cook the peels for 35 minutes or until completely softened. Top up with more water if needed.

2. Place the peels in a sieve and drain completely. Discard the water. Let cool to room temperature.

3. Push the peels through the sieve into a bowl, using the back of a spoon so that you end up with a purée. Measure out 1½ tablespoons (22 ml) and set aside (see note).

4. **MAKE THE TARTS:** In a large mixing bowl, whisk together the sugar, flour, and salt. Whisk in the egg yolks until well combined. Carefully whisk in the whipping cream in two additions, then the vanilla. Don't whisk too hard or fast—you don't want to overmix and aerate the cream or you'll end up with little soufflé tarts, which can collapse and be difficult to torch.

5. Strain the mixture through a fine-mesh sieve into a large measuring jug or bowl.

6. Stir 2 tablespoons (30 ml) of the brûlée mixture into the mandarin purée. (This will loosen it up a little and help the two mixtures to blend together more easily without overmixing.) Then stir the mandarin mixture into the brûlée mixture until just combined. Cover with plastic wrap and let rest in the fridge for at least 1 hour, and preferably overnight.

continued →

7. Spray or brush eight 4-inch (10 cm) tart rings with a neutral oil and place them on a large parchment-lined sheet pan.

8. Remove the pastry from the fridge and let it sit at room temperature for about 10 minutes.

9. On a lightly floured surface, using a floured rolling pin, gently roll out the pastry to an even thickness of about ⅛ inch (3 mm). (Rolling it out between two sheets of parchment paper makes life easier.)

10. Using a cookie cutter or a thin-rimmed glass, cut out eight 5-inch (13 cm) circles. Line each tart ring with the pastry, pressing it in well around the edges and bottom. Avoid leaving any air pockets between the pastry and the rings, and make sure there are no cracks where the brûlée filling can leak out. (If needed, gently combine the pastry scraps without overworking, then wrap and refrigerate for 30 minutes before rerolling and cutting. Discard any leftover pastry after rolling it the second time.)

11. Using a small knife, trim the excess pastry from above the sides of the tart rings so that the pastry is flush with the ring. Cover the rings with plastic wrap and refrigerate for 30 minutes.

12. Meanwhile, preheat the oven to 350°F (180°C), with a rack on the bottom rung.

13. Gently stir the brûlée filling, then pour it slowly into each tart ring. Fill the pastry right to the top or it will be challenging to torch later.

14. Bake for 25–30 minutes, rotating the pan a half turn after 12 minutes, until the pastry is golden brown and the filling has risen slightly and is firm when you gently wobble the pan. Let cool to room temperature for at least 30 minutes.

15. Carefully remove the tarts from the rings and place them one at a time on a large metal tray turned upside down (see note on page 24), ready to torch. Be careful not to turn the tarts upside down, as the filling is delicate.

16. Working with one tart at a time, lightly and evenly sprinkle it with some sugar—you only need a light coating to start. The secret to a good brûlée is all in how evenly you apply the sugar. Using a small blowtorch, gently wave the flame over the sugar until it begins to melt. Try not to get much color on the sugar at this point, and torch inward to avoid burning the pastry.

17. Sprinkle a second layer of sugar evenly on the top of the tart. Be very careful, as the molten sugar is very hot and will give you a terrible burn if it gets on your skin! Gently wave the blowtorch over the sugar again, evenly melting the sugar. You will start to see some color form as the sugar caramelizes.

18. Repeat a third and final time and torch until the sugar turns a light caramel color. Be careful not to over-torch the sugar, as burnt sugar tastes bitter and terrible.

19. Repeat steps 16–18 with the remaining tarts. This can be a tricky process and might take some practice.

20. Let the molten sugar cool slightly, then carefully use a spatula to transfer the tarts to a wire rack to cool completely, about 15 minutes.

These tarts are best eaten within 1 or 2 hours of torching; otherwise, the sugar starts to soften. If made ahead, prior to adding the sugar, they will keep in an airtight container in the fridge for 1–2 days; however, this will soften the pastry. Best to be on the safe side and eat them right away.

KITCHEN NOTE:

1. You may have some extra mandarin purée. This is a wonderful addition to stir-fries, stocks, roasts, or any other dish that would benefit from a delicious citrus essence. Keep it well wrapped in the freezer for up to a month and break off a piece as you need it.

Chocolate Peanut Butter Tart

1 recipe Chocolate Pastry
(page 236)

½ cup (125 ml) Dulce de
Leche (page 252)

½ cup (125 ml) crunchy
peanut butter

3 cups (540 g) semisweet
dark chocolate chips

2 cups (500 ml) whipping
cream

1 tsp pure vanilla extract

1 tsp cocoa powder, for
dusting

½ tsp flaky sea salt, for
sprinkling on top (or more
if desired)

I remember the first time I ate peanut M&M's. We didn't have them in Australia, but when we were on a camping trip in the U.S. when I was five, our campsite neighbors brought some over as a treat. To this day, my kids get me a big jar of peanut M&M's for Christmas, as they know these are my favorite! This tart is my amped-up, guest-worthy version of my favorite flavors. It is rich, so it goes far and is great for a crowd, as everyone needs only a sliver. As I experimented with the recipe, my son, Sam, suggested adding peanut butter to the dulce de leche. This, my friends, is why it's important to have your kids hanging around in the kitchen while you bake.

1. Spray or brush a 12-inch (30 cm) fluted tart tin with a neutral oil and line the bottom with parchment paper.

2. On a lightly floured surface, using a lightly floured rolling pin, roll the pastry into a 14-inch (35 cm) circle, about ⅛ inch (3 mm) thick. (You can use cocoa powder instead of flour to dust the pastry if you wish to avoid white streaks on the brown dough but be warned: it is much more work to clean up!)

3. Carefully roll the pastry onto the rolling pin and unroll it into the prepared pan. Gently press the bottom and sides of the pastry into the curves of the pan. Trim off the excess pastry. Refrigerate for 30 minutes.

4. Meanwhile, preheat the oven to 350°F (180°C).

5. Place a circle of parchment paper on the pastry crust and fill the crust with pie weights or dried beans. If you don't have either, use a fork to prick the bottom and sides of the crust all over.

6. Bake until the crust is just baked through, 15–20 minutes. (If you have pie weights, bake for closer to 20 minutes. If it's pricked with a fork, stick to 15 minutes.) Keep an eye on it. If you are using the fork method and you see it puff up, gently prick it again so it deflates. Let cool completely on a wire rack. If you are using pie weights, remove them.

7. In a small bowl, combine the dulce de leche and peanut butter. Spread over the base of the tart shell, using a small offset spatula. Refrigerate for 10–15 minutes.

8. Meanwhile, place the chocolate chips in a heatproof mixing bowl.

9. In a medium pot, combine the cream and vanilla. Bring to a rapid boil over high heat, stirring occasionally. As soon as the cream comes to a boil, it will begin to rise in the saucepan. Immediately pour it over the chocolate chips.

continued →

10. Leave the two ingredients alone for a minute or two, to get acquainted. This allows the chocolate to heat up, melt a little, and combine more quickly and thoroughly with the cream. Whisk to combine for about 1 minute or until the chocolate is completely melted (see note).

11. Pour the chocolate through a fine-mesh sieve into the tart shell and spread it out evenly by gently tapping the pan on the counter. Pop any air bubbles with a toothpick or a small paring knife. Let cool to room temperature, then refrigerate, uncovered, until completely set, about 2 hours.

12. Let sit at room temperature for about 20 minutes before serving. Dust with cocoa and sprinkle sea salt on top.

This tart will keep in an airtight container in the fridge for up to 3 days. I don't recommend freezing it.

KITCHEN NOTE:

1. I encourage people to use a whisk to combine the cream and the chocolate, but I always tell my staff to "stir it, don't whisk it!" Don't stir too hard or fast or you'll get lots of air bubbles, which can ruin the aesthetic of the smooth chocolate top.

Strawberry Cardamom Rhubarb Pie

1 recipe Sour Cream Pastry (page 237), cold

5 cups (650 g) chopped rhubarb (½-inch/1.2 cm pieces)

5 cups (650 g) chopped strawberries (½-inch/1.2 cm pieces)

1 cup (200 g) + 1 Tbsp granulated sugar, divided

2 Tbsp (20 g) all-purpose flour

2 Tbsp (15 g) cornstarch

1 Tbsp fresh lemon juice

2 tsp rosewater (optional)

2 tsp ground cardamom

1 tsp pure vanilla extract

½ tsp finely grated lemon zest

½ tsp ground cinnamon

½ tsp kosher salt

2 Tbsp (30 g) cold unsalted butter, cut into small pieces

1 egg, whisked with 1 Tbsp cold water to make an egg wash

Strawberry and rhubarb are a classic combination that we use often in the shop in tarts, pies, and galettes, or simply stewed and dolloped over custard or ice cream. Everything about this pie is so fragrant and reminiscent of summer, and the hint of cardamom adds a citrusy, earthy depth. Both sweet and sour, with the bright and fresh flavors of the season, it is something we look forward to bringing back year after year. Rhubarb is one of those fruits that easily takes on other flavors, so I often infuse it with sugar and rose-scented geranium leaves. The rosewater in this recipe stands in for that process, and if you can find some, I highly recommend it.

---

1. Divide the pastry into two even pieces and wrap well with plastic wrap. Refrigerate for at least 1 hour.

2. Preheat the oven to 375°F (190°C). Lightly spray or brush a 9-inch (23 cm) deep-dish pie plate with a neutral oil and place it on a parchment-lined rimmed sheet pan.

3. On a lightly floured surface, using a lightly floured rolling pin, roll out the first half of the pastry into an 11-inch (28 cm) circle, about ⅛ inch (3 mm) thick. Keep the other half in the fridge for now.

4. Carefully roll the pastry onto the rolling pin and unroll it into the pie plate. Gently press the bottom and sides of the pastry into the plate.

5. In a large bowl, combine the rhubarb, strawberries, 1 cup (200 g) sugar, flour, cornstarch, lemon juice, rosewater (if using), cardamom, vanilla, lemon zest, cinnamon, and salt. Transfer the mixture to the crust. Distribute the butter pieces evenly on top.

6. Roll out the second half of the pastry into a 12 × 10-inch (30 × 25 cm) rectangle, about ⅛ inch (3 mm) thick. Using a sharp knife and a ruler, cut fourteen strips of dough, each 10 inches (25 cm) long and about ¾ inch (2 cm) wide. Before crisscrossing the pastry strips over the pie, you can first chill the strips by laying them on parchment paper in the fridge for 10 minutes, which will make the crisscrossing process less messy and easier to fix.

continued →

7. To crisscross the strips, follow this process (scan the QR code below for a how-to video): Lay seven strips crosswise over the pie, leaving an even amount of space between each and letting the ends hang over the edge. Fold the first, third, fifth, and seventh strips halfway back on themselves. Lay one strip lengthwise along the center of the pie. Unfold the folded strips back over the pie so they are on top of the lengthwise strip. Fold the second, fourth, and sixth crosswise strips halfway back on themselves, so they are over the center lengthwise strip. Lay a second strip of dough lengthwise, to the left of the first lengthwise strip, and unfold the folded strips back over top. Continue this pattern of folding every second crosswise strip back, placing a lengthwise strip on top, working to the left edge of the pie then returning to the center and working to the right edge, and weaving the strips together until you've placed all fourteen strips.

8. Brush the edges of the bottom pastry with a little water, then pinch and crimp the edges of the pastry together to seal, trimming off any excess. Brush the egg wash carefully over the pastry. Sprinkle the extra tablespoon of sugar evenly over the top of the crust.

9. Bake for 50–60 minutes or until the crust is a deep golden brown and the fruit juice is bubbling at the edges. If the crust is getting too dark after 40 minutes or so, gently lay some foil over top. Let cool completely before serving. I recommend 4 hours for it to set up properly.

This pie will keep, covered, at room temperature for 2 days or in the fridge for up to 1 week. Or wrap tightly and freeze for up to 1 month; thaw in the fridge overnight before eating.

 Scan for crisscrossing tips

KITCHEN NOTES:

1. I don't suggest using frozen fruit for this recipe, as there would be too much liquid, which would make the pie very soggy.

2. Avoid using thick rhubarb stems, as they tend to be woody and tough. Choose slender, young rhubarb if possible.

Lemon Meringue Pie

2 cups (250 g) graham
cracker crumbs

⅓ cup (75 g) unsalted
butter, melted

1-2 Tbsp (15-30 ml) hot
water (100-110°F/38-43°C)

1 recipe Lemon Curd
(page 251), still warm

1 recipe Swiss Meringue
(page 241; see note)

Back in the day, lemon meringue pies were not what they are now. In those decades of convenience, the curd came from a box mix and was a chemical lemony flavor that was stiff and pale and lacked the creaminess we unknowingly craved. The meringue was a quick whisk of raw egg whites and a bit of granulated sugar—foamy and loose. The whole pie, piled high, went in under the broiler to brown a bit, creating a spotty, pale-brown skin of cooked egg white on top, the inside weepy and drooping, rapidly sogging up the store-bought crust. How things have changed! This version is creamy and lemony sweet and sour throughout, with a flaky, homemade crust beneath and piles of fluffy, thick torched meringue. We've come a long way, baby.

1. Spray or brush a 9-inch (23 cm) pie pan with a neutral oil.

2. In a medium bowl, combine the graham crumbs, butter, and 1 tablespoon of the hot water. Mix with a wooden spoon until combined. It should clump together when you squeeze it between your fingers. If it doesn't, add a bit more hot water.

3. Transfer the graham mixture into the prepared pan, bringing it up the sides to the edges of the pan. Press down with your fingertips until flat and even. Smooth out using the back of a large metal spoon, then place in the fridge for 30 minutes.

4. Meanwhile, preheat the oven to 350°F (180°C).

5. Bake the base until firm, about 10 minutes. Let cool on a wire rack.

6. Pour the warm curd into the tart shell. It should come up to just below the rim. Cover loosely with plastic wrap and refrigerate for at least 1 hour and up to 1 day.

7. Spread the meringue evenly over top of the pie. Give the pie some texture by dabbing a spatula onto the meringue and lifting it off, creating little spikes. Work quickly, as the meringue will begin to collapse after about 10 minutes.

8. Using a small kitchen blowtorch, evenly brown the meringue all over to give it some flavor and visual appeal.

This pie will keep in an airtight container in the fridge for about a week. I don't recommend freezing it.

KITCHEN NOTES:

1. If you find the Swiss meringue is losing its volume and becoming a bit too runny, whisk it again until it has regained its volume, 3-5 minutes.

2. If you like, after the lemon curd has set and before adding the Swiss meringue, top the pie with a handful of raspberries, blueberries, or another favorite berry.

Frangipane Tart

with Cinnamon Poached Pears

Cinnamon Poached Pears

2 cups (500 ml) pure apple juice

½ cup (100 g) dark brown sugar, lightly packed

2 cinnamon sticks

2 pears (such as Bartlett, Anjou, or Bosc)

Frangipane Filling

½ cup (115 g) unsalted butter, at room temperature

½ cup (100 g) granulated sugar

2 eggs, at room temperature

1 cup (120 g) almond flour, lightly packed

1 Tbsp all-purpose flour

¼ tsp kosher salt

2 tsp brandy (optional)

1 tsp pure vanilla extract

1 recipe Sweet Pastry (page 236), cold

1 tsp icing sugar, for dusting

As a kid, I loved the flavor of almonds, especially when they were made into a sweet treat such as marzipan or frangipane. And pears—an autumn staple in my house these days—always remind me of backpacking through France in my early twenties over the fall season, when pears were at their peak. Just the scent of a fresh pear brings those memories flooding back. Now, at Crust, we've always got frangipane in some dessert or another, and often use pears, as they are a lovely fall fruit. Put these two together, and you've got a decadent (and nostalgia-inducing) dessert.

1. **MAKE THE PEARS:** In a medium saucepan over medium-high heat, combine the apple juice, brown sugar, and cinnamon sticks and bring to a simmer, then lower the heat to low. Cover the pot with a tight-fitting lid and continue to simmer for 5 minutes. Turn off the heat and, leaving the lid on, let the cinnamon infuse the liquid for 15 minutes.

2. Peel the pears and cut into quarters. Carefully and neatly remove the core so the quarters stay intact. Gently place the pears in the hot cinnamon liquid and turn the heat to medium. Cook for 20–25 minutes or until the pears have turned translucent and a sharp knife easily slides into them. Remove from the heat and let the pears cool completely in the liquid.

3. **MAKE THE FILLING:** In a stand mixer, combine the butter and granulated sugar. Using the paddle attachment, mix on medium-high speed until the butter is pale and the consistency resembles mayonnaise, 2–4 minutes.

4. Turn the mixer down to low speed and add 1 egg. Combine thoroughly with the butter mixture before adding the second egg. Take your time with this step.

5. Add the almond flour, all-purpose flour, and salt and mix on medium-low speed until combined. Add the brandy (if using) and vanilla. Scrape down the sides of the bowl to ensure there are no pockets of unmixed butter or flour. Gently fold in any you missed. Pulse the mixer a few times until all ingredients are well mixed.

6. **ASSEMBLE THE TART:** Spray or brush a 12-inch (30 cm) fluted tart tin with a neutral oil. (A tart tin with a removable base will be very helpful here, but if you don't have one, a regular one will do.)

7. Remove the pastry from the fridge and let sit at room temperature for 5 minutes.

continued →

8. On a lightly floured surface, using a lightly floured rolling pin, gently roll out the pastry into a 13-inch (33 cm) circle, about ¼ inch (6 mm) thick.

9. Carefully roll the pastry onto the rolling pin, and unroll it into the prepared tin. Gently press the bottom and sides of the pastry into the curves of the tin. Avoid leaving any air pockets between the pastry and the tin, and make sure there are no cracks where the filling can leak out. Trim off the excess pastry. Refrigerate for about 20 minutes.

10. Meanwhile, preheat the oven to 350°F (180°C).

11. Place the tart tin on a parchment-lined rimmed sheet pan. Fill the tart shell evenly with the frangipane to a bit more than halfway up the shell.

12. Remove the pears from the cooking liquid and pat dry with paper towels. Slice each pear quarter crosswise into 8–10 slices. Carefully transfer the sliced pears to the tart, arranging them decoratively on top of the frangipane. (A small offset spatula is helpful for picking up and placing the pear pieces.)

13. Bake for 45–55 minutes or until the pastry is golden brown and the frangipane has started to puff up a little. The top should be a deep golden brown. Let cool to room temperature in the tin on a wire rack.

14. To serve, remove the tart from the pan and dust lightly with the icing sugar.

   This tart is best eaten at room temperature. It can be kept in an airtight container at room temperature for 2 days, in the fridge for up to 1 week, or in the freezer for up to 1 month.

KITCHEN NOTES:

1. The pastry and pears can be made up to 3 days in advance and kept in airtight containers in the fridge. Frangipane can be kept in an airtight container in the fridge for up to 2 weeks, or in the freezer for up to 6 weeks.

2. If you don't have cinnamon sticks, you can substitute 2 teaspoons of ground cinnamon.

Peach Melba Hand Pies

Pastry Cream

¼ cup (50 g) granulated sugar

1 Tbsp cornstarch

1 Tbsp all-purpose flour

1 egg

1 cup (250 ml) whole milk

½ tsp pure vanilla extract

Pies

1 recipe Sour Cream Pastry (page 237), cold

2 large ripe freestone peaches

24 raspberries

1 egg, whisked with 2 tsp cold water to make an egg wash

3 Tbsp (36 g) coarse sugar, to sprinkle (approx.)

When I turned nine, my parents took me for my very first fancy restaurant experience. My eyes were wide as I took it all in, my senses at full attention. The chef was on the Australian Culinary Olympic team, which absolutely fascinated me, and I began to feel something wonderful stirring deep inside my soul for this unfamiliar environment, though I didn't know just what that was. I can't recall what I ate for dinner, but I do remember the dessert menu: floating islands of meringue on crème anglaise, Crêpes Suzette, Bombe Alaska, and, of course, Peach Melba—a dish of stewed peaches and raspberry sauce served over vanilla ice cream. I'll never forget that monumental birthday, and I'll never forget Peach Melba. This is my version of the classic dessert, modernized and wrapped in pastry.

1. **MAKE THE PASTRY CREAM:** In a bowl, whisk together the granulated sugar, cornstarch, and flour. Add 1 egg and whisk until well mixed and smooth. Add the milk and whisk until well combined.

2. Transfer the mixture to a small saucepan over medium heat. Cook, whisking continuously, until the mixture thickens and comes to a gentle boil, 5–7 minutes. Be patient, and don't be tempted to turn the heat up too high, as it can burn quickly. Make sure the mixture doesn't stick to the bottom of the pan. Remove the pan from the heat and stir in the vanilla.

3. Pour the pastry cream through a fine-mesh sieve into a small bowl. Immediately cover with plastic wrap, ensuring the plastic touches the pastry cream surface so it doesn't form a skin. Let cool for 30–60 minutes, then refrigerate until ready to use, up to 3 days.

4. **MAKE THE PIES:** Line a large sheet pan with plastic wrap.

5. On a lightly floured surface, using a lightly floured rolling pin, roll out the pastry into a 12 × 24-inch (30 × 60 cm) rectangle, just under ¼ inch (6 mm) thick.

6. Using a 6-inch (15 cm) round pastry cutter or a thin-rimmed glass (don't tell my wife, but at home I use her favorite vase!), dip the cutter in a bit of flour and cut eight circles out of the pastry. Make sure your pastry disks do not have cracks in them. If they do, pinch and work the dough gently to mend the cracks. (If you can't get eight disks out of your first roll of pastry, gather the scraps and lightly form them into a flat disk. Wrap with plastic wrap and refrigerate for 20 minutes before rerolling and cutting again. Discard any scraps after that.)

7. Place the pastry disks on the sheet pan. If you need to layer them, layer plastic wrap between them. Wrap the whole pan well with plastic wrap and refrigerate for 1 hour.

continued →

8. Line two sheet pans with parchment paper. Arrange four pastry disks on each pan, leaving plenty of space between them. Gently reroll each disk to 6 inches (15 cm) in diameter if they have shrunk a bit while resting.

9. Place about 1½ tablespoons (22 ml) of chilled pastry cream slightly off-center on each disk.

10. Cut the peaches in half and discard the pits. Cut each half in half again. Slice each quarter lengthwise into three pieces. (The peaches don't need to be peeled, but can be if you prefer.)

11. On each disk, fan three peach slices on top of the pastry cream, leaving a 1-inch (2.5 cm) border around the edges. Top with three raspberries.

12. Moisten the border of one-half of each pastry disk with the egg wash to help the pastry stick together. Reserve the remaining egg wash.

13. Fold the disk in half over the peaches and berries to create a semicircle. Working around the border, pinch the edges together, crimping as you go with your fingertips or a fork, making sure the seam is sealed.

14. Set the pies on one sheet pan and refrigerate for 15–30 minutes (or up to 24 hours, covered, if you want to bake them later).

15. Meanwhile, preheat the oven to 400°F (200°C).

16. Separate the pies between the two sheet pans, with four on each pan and plenty of room in between. Gently brush the reserved egg wash over each pie. Sprinkle coarse sugar generously over each. Cut three slashes, about 2 inches (5 cm) long, in the top of each pie.

17. Bake for 25–30 minutes, rotating the pans after 12 minutes, until the pastry is deep golden brown and the filling is bubbling. Let cool to room temperature before eating. Be cautious, as the filling remains hot for quite some time.

These pies are best eaten the same day they are made, but can be kept for a few days in an airtight container in the fridge or unbaked in the freezer for up to 3 weeks. Thaw frozen pies for 1–2 hours at room temperature before baking.

KITCHEN NOTES:

1. Use dark brown sugar, good-quality bourbon, and good-quality vanilla extract for the best flavor.

2. These tarts are delicious at room temperature but are also delectably sticky and chewy straight out of the fridge.

Chocolate, Bourbon, and Pecan Butter Tarts

4 eggs

1½ cups (300 g) dark brown sugar, lightly packed

½ tsp kosher salt

2 Tbsp (30 ml) good-quality bourbon

1 Tbsp pure vanilla extract

2 tsp fresh lemon juice

1 recipe Sweet Pastry (page 236), cold

1 cup (120 g) pecan halves or roughly chopped macadamia nuts

½ cup (90 g) semisweet dark chocolate chips

Ever since Crust opened, these tarts have been a huge hit, and we serve them daily, always selling out, with the end-of-the-day stragglers squeezing in before we close the doors for the night, hoping they get lucky enough to grab the last one or two. I fill these decadent tarts with pecans, but in Australia, I would make them with macadamia nuts, which are much more easily accessible there. (You certainly can do that here if you have access to macadamias!) Either way, buttery, crunchy nuts mixed with chocolate, caramel, and bourbon make for a magnificent treat, and these tarts are great for sharing, as they are quite rich.

1. In a large mixing bowl, whisk together the eggs and sugar until well combined. Add the salt, bourbon, vanilla, and lemon juice and continue whisking gently. You want to dissolve the sugar, but don't want to add too much air to the mixture. Cover and refrigerate for at least 30 minutes or up to 1 week.

2. Lightly brush or spray eight 4-inch (10 cm) fluted tart tins with a neutral oil. Line a large rimmed sheet pan with parchment paper.

3. On a lightly floured surface, using a lightly floured rolling pin, roll out the pastry to about ⅛ inch (3 mm) thick.

4. Using a cookie cutter, or a thin glass, cut out eight 4½-inch (11 cm) disks. Tuck a disk into each tart tin, pressing it well into all the curves and making sure there are no cracks or air pockets. Ensure the pastry comes right up to the top of each tin, as it will shrink slightly as it bakes. Set the tins on the prepared sheet pan, cover with plastic wrap, and refrigerate for 1 hour.

5. Meanwhile, preheat the oven to 350°F (180°C).

6. Divide the pecans and chocolate chips evenly among the tarts, then fill each tart with the bourbon caramel mixture. Depending on the depth of your tart tins, you may have some filling left over (spoon it over ice cream!).

7. Bake for 20–25 minutes or until the pastry is golden brown and the filling is cooked through and has puffed a little. Transfer the tins to a wire rack and let cool for at least 20 minutes, then carefully remove the tarts from the tins. Return the tarts to the rack and let cool completely before serving.

These tarts will keep in an airtight container at room temperature for 2 days or in the fridge for up to 1 week.

Toffee Poached Apple Pie
with Salted Almond Crumble

½ recipe Basic Pastry (page 235), cold

1 recipe Toffee Poached Apples (page 248)

2 Tbsp (15 g) cornstarch

1 recipe Salted Almond Crumble (page 246)

Lightly sweetened whipped cream, to garnish

We often use this delicious combination of flavors for our Danish pastries at Crust. The salty almond topping balances the deep caramel sweetness, and that, combined with the earthy depth of cooked apples, makes it hard to resist. This next-level apple pie is a great way to use up autumn apples from the trees that occupy many Canadian backyards. Be careful about taste-testing the crumble. It's addictive, and you won't be able to stop!

1. Lightly spray or brush a 9-inch (23 cm) springform pan with a neutral oil and line it with parchment paper.

2. On a lightly floured surface, using a lightly floured rolling pin, roll out the pastry into a 12-inch (30 cm) circle, about ¼ inch (6 mm) thick. Cut out an 11-inch (28 cm) circle.

3. Carefully roll the pastry onto the rolling pin and unroll it into the prepared springform pan. Gently press the bottom of the pastry to expel any air pockets, and tuck it right into the edges of the pan. Make sure the pastry comes up evenly around the sides. Refrigerate for 15 minutes.

4. Meanwhile, preheat the oven to 350°F (180°C).

5. Drain the poached apples, reserving ⅓ cup (75 ml) of the poaching liquid.

6. In a small bowl, whisk together the cornstarch and the poaching liquid.

7. Place the apples in a bowl and pour in the cornstarch mixture. Stir gently to combine well.

8. Place the springform pan on a parchment-lined rimmed sheet pan. Pour the apples evenly into the pastry shell, pressing them down gently to ensure the top is flat and even. Cover evenly with the crumble, patting it down gently with your fingertips.

9. Bake for 45–55 minutes or until the pastry and the crumble are a deep golden brown and the apples are bubbling at the edges. Let cool completely on a wire rack. Serve garnished with whipped cream.

   This pie will keep in an airtight container in the fridge for up to 4 days or in the freezer for up to 1 month. Thaw the frozen pie in the fridge overnight and reheat in the oven, if desired, at 350°F (180°C) until warmed through, about 25 minutes.

KITCHEN NOTES:

1. You can make this pie in a deep-dish pie dish if you prefer.

2. If you notice that the apples are not bubbling but the pastry and crumble are looking too dark during the baking process, tent the pie loosely with foil.

KITCHEN NOTES: 1. To reheat cold quiche, cover it with foil and bake in a 300°F
                        (150°C) oven for 35-45 minutes or until hot in the center.

Zucchini, Dill, and Feta Quiche

1 recipe Savory Pastry
(page 238), at room
temperature

1 Tbsp olive oil

1 small (100 g) white
onion, cut into ½-inch
(1.2 cm) dice

4 eggs

2 cups (500 ml) half-and-
half cream

1 tsp kosher salt

½ tsp ground white pepper

¼ tsp ground nutmeg

¼ tsp cayenne pepper

2 cups (100 g) baby
spinach, stems removed

2 medium (200 g) green
zucchini, cut into ½-inch
(1.2 cm) cubes

1 cup (150 g) crumbled
feta cheese (½-inch/1.2 cm
chunks)

¼ cup (5 g) roughly
chopped fresh dill

In my previous life as a chef, I was very passionate about growing my own produce. One year, I found myself challenged by an excess of zucchini. One of the recipes I came up with was a feta, dill, and zucchini fritter, which we served as an appetizer. In my baking, I often take inspiration from my chef days, and this combination is so good with the creamy egg custard of a decadent quiche.

1. Spray or brush a 9-inch (23 cm) deep-dish quiche pan with a neutral oil.

2. On a lightly floured surface, using a lightly floured rolling pin, roll out the pastry to about ⅛-inch (3 mm) thickness. Make sure it is evenly rolled, to help it bake evenly.

3. Carefully roll the pastry onto the rolling pin and unroll it into the prepared quiche pan. Gently press the pastry into the bottom and sides of the tin pan, tucking it right into the edges and making sure there are no cracks or air pockets between the pastry and the pan. Let the excess pastry drape over the sides of the pan. Refrigerate for 30–60 minutes to allow the pastry to relax.

4. Meanwhile, preheat the oven to 400°F (200°C). Place the quiche pan on a parchment-lined rimmed sheet pan in case of spills. Using a fork, prick the bottom and sides of the shell all over.

5. Bake until nicely golden, 10–15 minutes. You want the crust to be fully baked at this point. Keep an eye on it; if it puffs up while baking, gently prick it with the fork to deflate it. (Don't worry if it cracks while baking; see the note on page 54 for how to patch it up.) Remove from the oven and lower the oven temperature to 325°F (160°C).

6. Meanwhile, in a sauté pan over medium-low heat, heat the olive oil. Cook the onion, stirring occasionally, until it's translucent, 7–10 minutes. Adjust the heat as needed so the onion does not brown. Remove from the heat and set aside.

7. In a medium bowl, whisk the eggs together. Briskly whisk in the cream, salt, white pepper, nutmeg, and cayenne until well combined.

8. Cover the crust evenly with the spinach, followed by the onions and zucchini. Sprinkle the feta and dill evenly over top. Carefully fill the quiche with the egg mixture, as full as you can.

9. Bake for 50–60 minutes or until the custard is set and light golden brown on top and the quiche has risen a bit. Let cool for 10 minutes.

10. Using a small serrated knife, trim off the excess pastry. Rub the cut part of the pastry with your palm to disguise where you cut it. Serve hot, warm, or cold.

This quiche will keep in an airtight container in the fridge for up to 4 days. I don't recommend freezing it.

Bacon, Tomato, and Smoked Cheddar Quiche

1 recipe Savory Pastry (page 238), at room temperature

⅓ cup (100 g) diced smoked bacon (1-inch/2.5 cm dice)

1 small (100 g) white onion, cut into ½-inch (1.2 cm) dice

4 eggs

2 cups (500 ml) half-and-half cream

1 tsp kosher salt

½ tsp ground white pepper

½ tsp ground nutmeg

¼ tsp cayenne pepper

1 cup (50 g) baby spinach, stems removed

½ cup (100 g) halved cherry tomatoes

1½ cup (135 g) grated smoked Cheddar cheese

In the shop, we make our quiches individual-sized so people can carry them away easily. This flavor is probably our most popular (it is my favorite!); we sell hundreds per week. You can only imagine the kitchen assembly line that results in hundreds of quiches. I love offering savory treats at Crust alongside our sweets, and this one is full of smoky, deep flavors with a little hit of bright acidity from the tomatoes. We have a ton of customers who favor these for breakfast, as well as for lunch.

1. Spray or brush a 9-inch (23 cm) deep-dish quiche pan with a neutral oil.

2. On a lightly floured surface, using a lightly floured rolling pin, roll out the pastry to about ⅛-inch (3 mm) thickness. Make sure it is evenly rolled, to help it bake evenly.

3. Carefully roll the pastry onto the rolling pin and unroll it into the prepared quiche pan. Gently press the pastry into the bottom and sides of the pan, tucking it right into the edges and making sure there are no cracks or air pockets between the pastry and the pan. Let the excess pastry drape over the sides of the pan. Refrigerate for 30–60 minutes to allow the pastry to relax.

4. Meanwhile, preheat the oven to 400°F (200°C).

5. Place the quiche pan on a parchment-lined rimmed sheet pan in case of spills. Using a fork, prick the bottom and sides of the shell all over.

6. Bake until nicely golden, 10–15 minutes. You want the crust to be fully baked at this point. Keep an eye on it; if it puffs up while baking, gently prick it with the fork to deflate it. (Don't worry if it cracks while baking; see the notes for how to patch it up.) Remove from the oven and lower the oven temperature to 325°F (160°C).

7. Meanwhile, in a medium sauté pan over medium heat, cook the bacon and the onion, stirring occasionally, until the onion is translucent and the bacon is cooked through, about 10 minutes. Adjust the heat as needed so the onion doesn't brown. Using a slotted spoon, transfer the bacon and onions to a small bowl, allowing any excess fat to drain off. Discard the fat.

8. In a medium bowl, whisk the eggs together. Briskly whisk in the cream, salt, white pepper, nutmeg, and cayenne until well combined.

continued →

9. Cover the crust evenly with the spinach, followed by the bacon mixture, then the tomatoes, cut side up, then the Cheddar. Carefully fill the quiche with the egg mixture, as full as you can. (You may have a wee bit left over, depending on the depth of your pan. Pour any excess into a buttered small ramekin and bake it along with the quiche or fry it up for a snack!)

10. Bake for 50–60 minutes or until the custard is set and light golden brown on top and the quiche has risen a bit. Let cool for 10 minutes.

11. Using a small serrated knife, trim off the excess pastry. Rub the cut part of the pastry with your palm to disguise where you cut it. Serve hot, warm, or cold.

This quiche will keep in an airtight container in the fridge for up to 4 days. I don't recommend freezing it.

KITCHEN NOTES:

1. Instead of half-and-half, you can substitute whole milk and whipping cream in a 50:50 ratio.

2. If your crust cracks while you are prebaking it, don't panic! Make a smooth paste by mixing 1 tablespoon of flour with 1 tablespoon of water. Use your fingers to patch up and fill any cracks, and return it to the oven for a minute or so to set.

Mushroom, Pesto, and Goat Cheese Quiche

SERVES 8–10

1 recipe Savory Pastry (page 238), at room temperature

1 Tbsp olive oil

1 small (100 g) white onion, cut into ½-inch (1.2 cm) dice

2 cups (200 g) sliced button mushrooms

1 pinch + ½ tsp kosher salt, divided

4 eggs

2 cups (500 ml) half-and-half cream

½ tsp kosher salt

½ tsp ground white pepper

½ tsp ground nutmeg

¼ tsp cayenne pepper

2 cups (100 g) baby spinach, stems removed

½ cup (50 g) crumbled goat cheese

2 Tbsp (40 g) good-quality basil pesto

2 Tbsp (60 g) raw pine nuts

We have a customer who is a longtime fan of our quiches. Every week, she comes in and orders a dozen individual ones for her family to enjoy in their lunches at work and school. It was her enthusiasm for and love of our quiches that inspired me to create a selection of new and interesting flavor combinations, and to offer a few more savory items for our customers to take away for breakfast, lunch, or dinner. This is what keeps me excited about the shop and baking and creating things for all our lovely customers. While it is true that I am a baker, the chef in me still takes great pleasure in creating little savory, flavorful handheld treats!

1. Spray or brush a 9-inch (23 cm) deep-dish quiche pan with a neutral oil.

2. On a lightly floured surface, using a lightly floured rolling pin, roll out the pastry to about ⅛-inch (3 mm) thickness. Make sure it is evenly rolled, to help it bake evenly.

3. Carefully roll the pastry onto the rolling pin and unroll it into the prepared quiche pan. Gently press the pastry into the bottom and sides of the pan, tucking it right into the edges and making sure there are no cracks or air pockets between the pastry and the pan. Let the excess drape over the sides of the pan. (This method prevents the pastry from shrinking and sliding down the inside of the pan. You will have perfect crust every time!) Refrigerate for 30–60 minutes to allow the pastry to relax.

4. Meanwhile, preheat the oven to 400°F (200°C).

5. Place the quiche pan on a parchment-lined rimmed sheet pan in case of spills. Using a fork, prick the bottom and sides of the shell all over.

6. Bake until nicely golden, 10–15 minutes. You want the crust to be fully baked at this point. Keep an eye on it; if it puffs up while baking, gently prick it with the fork to deflate it. (Don't worry if it cracks while baking; see note on page 54 for how to patch it up.) Remove from the oven and lower the oven temperature to 325°F (160°C).

7. Meanwhile, in a sauté pan over medium-low heat, heat the olive oil. Cook the onion, mushrooms, and a pinch of salt, stirring occasionally, until the mushroom juice has evaporated and the onion is translucent, 10–15 minutes. Adjust the heat as needed so the onion does not brown. Remove from the heat and set aside.

continued →

8. In a medium bowl, whisk the eggs together. Briskly whisk in the cream, ½ tsp salt, white pepper, nutmeg, and cayenne until well combined.

9. Cover the crust evenly with the spinach, followed by the onion and mushroom mixture. Crumble the goat cheese over top, drizzle with the pesto, then sprinkle with the pine nuts. Carefully fill the quiche with the egg mixture, as full as you can.

10. Bake for 50–60 minutes or until the custard is set and light golden brown on top and the quiche has risen a bit. Let cool for 10 minutes.

11. Using a small serrated knife, trim off the excess pastry. Rub the cut part of the pastry with your palm to disguise where you cut it. (It's a very different technique, but it works well!) Serve hot, warm, or cold.

This quiche will keep in an airtight container in the fridge for up to 4 days. I don't recommend freezing it.

Muffins, Scones, and Squares

"It looked like the world was covered in a
cobbler crust of brown sugar and cinnamon."

SARAH ADDISON ALLEN

Toffee Poached Apple Muffins

with Salted Almond Crumble

2 cups (300 g) + 1 Tbsp all-purpose flour, divided

½ cup (100 g) granulated sugar

2 tsp baking powder

1 tsp ground cinnamon

¼ tsp kosher salt

1 cup (250 ml) buttermilk

⅔ cup (150 ml) vegetable oil

1 tsp pure vanilla extract

1 egg

1½ cups (375 g) Toffee Poached Apples (page 248), drained and cut into ½-inch (1.2 cm) pieces

1 recipe Salted Almond Crumble (page 246)

1 tsp icing sugar (optional)

One of the things I love most about Vancouver Island living is the plenitude of little honor-system farm stands sprinkled throughout the rural neighborhoods. People will put out a selection of their eggs, fruit, flowers, or freshly picked herbs, and you can drop by anytime, leave some cash in a box, and take your goods. Just like that. And through the seasons, we can open our front door and find a sack of zucchini or a pumpkin or a dozen eggs, never really sure which generous neighbor they came from. All of this nurtures the farm boy in me and warms my heart, reminding me of home. A common front porch fruit around here is apples, as there are so often way too many for one family to consume or preserve. Try this recipe if you open your door one autumn day to find a sack of apples from a kind anonymous friend.

1. Preheat the oven to 375°F (190°C). Place paper muffin liners in a 12-cup muffin tin.

2. Using a fine-mesh sieve, sift 2 cups (300 g) flour into a stand mixer bowl and add the granulated sugar, baking powder, cinnamon, and salt.

3. In a large measuring jug, combine the buttermilk, oil, vanilla, and egg. Whisk together or emulsify with an immersion blender to combine well.

4. Pour the wet ingredients into the dry ingredients. Using the paddle attachment, mix on low speed until just combined, about 10 seconds. Stop the mixer and scrape down the sides of the bowl with a spatula to ensure everything has been incorporated.

5. Turn the speed to medium and mix for another 10–15 seconds only. The mixture should be combined and smooth, like a thick pancake batter.

6. Sprinkle the remaining tablespoon of flour over the poached apples, then gently mix them into the batter with a wide spatula. Avoid overmixing the batter and breaking up the apples.

7. Divide the batter evenly among the prepared muffin cups, making sure each muffin has the same amount of apple. Sprinkle about 2 tablespoons (30 ml) of salted almond crumble on top of each muffin. Gently pat the crumble down to make sure it doesn't fall off while cooking.

8. Bake for 25–30 minutes or until the muffins are golden brown on top and a skewer inserted in the center of a muffin comes out clean. Let cool completely in the tin on a wire rack. Dust the muffins with icing sugar (if using) before serving.

These muffins are best eaten fresh, but will keep in an airtight container in the fridge for up to 3 days or wrapped individually in the freezer for up to 1 month.

Blackberry Cinnamon Oat Muffins

2 cups (300 g) + 1 tsp
all-purpose flour, divided

⅓ cup (70 g) granulated
sugar

⅓ cup (67 g) light brown
sugar, lightly packed

2 tsp baking powder

1½ tsp ground cinnamon

½ tsp finely grated
orange zest

¼ tsp kosher salt

1 cup (250 ml) whole milk

¾ cup (175 ml) vegetable oil

2 tsp fresh lemon juice

2 tsp pure vanilla extract

1 egg

2 cups (250 g) fresh
blackberries (or frozen,
thawed and drained)

Crumble Topping

1 cup (90 g) rolled oats

⅓ cup (70 g) dark brown
sugar, lightly packed

⅓ cup (50 g) all-purpose
flour

¼ cup (60 g) unsalted
butter, melted

1 tsp ground cinnamon

¼ tsp kosher salt

¼ tsp baking powder

Where I grew up in Australia, there were wild blackberry bushes everywhere you looked. When I moved to Canada, I was delighted to find the familiar thorny bushes in absolute abundance, in backyards, parks, and even on the roadside, where anyone could grab a bucket and help themselves. Each year, my kids and I pick them to our heart's content, freezing bag after bag so we can enjoy these sweet-sour berries all year long. These are some of my favorite muffins to use up our seemingly never-ending blackberry stash.

1. Preheat the oven to 375°F (190°C). Place paper muffin liners in a 12-cup muffin tin.

2. In a stand mixer (or a large bowl), combine 2 cups (300 g) flour, both sugars, baking powder, cinnamon, orange zest, and salt. Using the paddle attachment, beat on low speed until blended, about 1 minute. (If you are not using a stand mixer, beat with a hand mixer or vigorously with a wooden spoon until combined.)

3. In a large measuring jug, combine the milk, oil, lemon juice, vanilla, and egg. Whisk briskly or emulsify with an immersion blender to combine well.

4. Pour the wet ingredients into the dry ingredients and mix on low speed until just combined, about 20 seconds. Turn the speed up to medium and mix for another 10–20 seconds. The mixture should be combined and smooth, like a thick pancake batter. Pulse the mixer on high speed quickly once or twice, to make sure all the ingredients are combined properly.

5. Sprinkle the remaining teaspoon of flour over the blackberries. Remove the bowl from the stand and gently fold in the blackberries.

6. Divide the batter evenly among the prepared muffin cups.

7. **MAKE THE CRUMBLE:** In a medium mixing bowl, combine the oats, brown sugar, flour, butter, cinnamon, salt, and baking powder. Mix together until well combined, then rub the mixture together using your fingertips to create a textured crumble.

8. Divide the crumble mixture evenly among the muffins, pressing it gently into the batter to ensure it sticks to the tops of the muffins as they bake.

9. Bake for 20–25 minutes or until the muffins have risen and a skewer inserted in the center comes out clean. Let cool completely in the tin on a wire rack.

These muffins are best eaten fresh, but will keep in an airtight container in the fridge for up to 3 days or wrapped individually in the freezer for up to 1 month.

KITCHEN NOTES:

1. You can make the muffin batter 1-2 days ahead of time and keep it covered in the fridge until you are ready to bake. Let the batter warm to room temperature, add the berries, then bake.

2. You can substitute blueberries or raspberries, or use a combination. My wife loves to add about ½ cup (90 g) dark chocolate chips when she makes them. Maybe that's why the kids like hers better than mine!

KITCHEN NOTES:

1. Make sure the berries are kept frozen right until the last minute before adding them to your batter. If you let them thaw, they will bleed into the batter and turn the muffins blue.

Blueberry Yogurt
Lemon Zest Muffins

2 cups (300 g) + 1 tsp all-purpose flour, divided

⅔ cup (130 g) + 2 Tbsp (25 g) granulated sugar, divided

2 tsp baking powder

¼ tsp kosher salt

⅔ cup (150 ml) whole milk

⅔ cup (150 ml) vegetable oil

¼ cup (60 ml) full-fat unsweetened plain Greek yogurt

2 tsp finely grated lemon zest

2 tsp fresh lemon juice

1 tsp pure vanilla extract

1 egg

1½ cups (190 g) frozen blueberries, divided (see note)

Muffins are always a bestseller at Crust, and when I see the lineup of customers outside the shop every morning at 8 a.m., I know muffins will be flying out the door. (Along with croissants and pastries! But mostly muffins.) The best thing about muffins is that you can use whatever fruit, spice, and topping you like. This particular recipe is one I've used since I was an apprentice at the Capital Parkroyal Hotel in Canberra, at the age of sixteen, where I learned to make these muffins. Tried and true goes far in this business, and this is one recipe I will have in my back pocket for life.

1. Preheat the oven to 375°F (190°C). Place paper muffin liners in a 12-cup muffin tin.

2. Using a fine-mesh sieve, sift 2 cups (300 g) flour, ⅔ cup (135 g) sugar, and the baking powder and salt into a stand mixer bowl (or a large bowl).

3. In a large measuring jug, combine the milk, oil, yogurt, lemon zest, lemon juice, vanilla, and egg. Whisk briskly or emulsify with an immersion blender to combine well.

4. Pour the wet ingredients into the dry ingredients. Using the paddle attachment, mix on low speed until combined, about 20 seconds. Stop the mixer and scrape down the sides of the bowl with a spatula to ensure everything has been incorporated. (If you are not using a stand mixer, beat with a hand mixer or vigorously with a wooden spoon until combined and smooth.)

5. Turn the speed to medium-high and mix for another 5–10 seconds only. The mixture should be combined and smooth, like a thick pancake batter.

6. Toss 1 cup (125 g) of the frozen blueberries with the remaining teaspoon of flour (so they don't sink to the bottom of the muffins), then gently mix them into the batter with a spatula, reserving the remaining berries. Avoid overmixing the batter.

7. Divide the batter evenly among the prepared muffin cups, making sure each muffin has around the same number of blueberries. Divide the remaining blueberries evenly among the muffins, pushing them gently into the batter. Sprinkle the tops evenly with the remaining 2 tablespoons (25 g) of sugar.

8. Bake for 25–30 minutes or until the muffins have risen and a skewer inserted in the center of a muffin comes out clean. Let cool completely in the tin on a wire rack.

These muffins are best eaten fresh, but will keep in an airtight container in the fridge for up to 3 days or wrapped individually in the freezer for up to 1 month.

Banana and Macadamia Muffins

with Dulce de Leche

2 cups (300 g) all-purpose flour

2 tsp baking powder

¼ tsp kosher salt

1 cup (120 g) macadamia nuts, roughly chopped, divided

1 cup (250 g) mashed extra-ripe bananas (about 2 large)

⅓ cup (70 g) granulated sugar

⅓ cup (70 g) dark brown sugar, lightly packed

⅓ cup (75 ml) vegetable oil

1 egg

1 tsp pure vanilla extract

⅓ cup (75 g) unsalted butter

⅔ cup (150 ml) cold whole milk

2 tsp fresh lemon juice

1 recipe Dulce de Leche (page 252), divided

1 small banana, sliced into 12 coins

1 tsp icing sugar

Macadamias are an indigenous Australian tree nut and are used a lot in baking, or are simply roasted and salted for snacking. When I was a kid, we used to pick them from the trees and eat them raw, sometimes smashing our fingers as we tried to crack open their rock-hard shells with a hammer. I love this combination of creamy, crunchy nuts with sweet banana and caramel as a mid-morning snack with coffee, or even for breakfast on particularly fast-paced days. The caramel makes it decadent, with a depth of flavor that some may relate more to dessert, but I have no issue with eating dessert for breakfast!

1. Preheat the oven to 375°F (190°C). Place paper muffin liners in a 12-cup muffin tin.

2. Using a fine-mesh sieve, sift the flour, baking powder, and salt into a medium bowl. Stir in half of the macadamia nuts.

3. Place the bananas, granulated sugar, and brown sugar in a stand mixer bowl (or a large bowl). Using the paddle attachment, mix on medium speed for about 10 seconds or until the bananas have broken up into small pieces and it looks like a chunky mess. (If you are not using a stand mixer, beat with a hand mixer or vigorously with a wooden spoon.)

4. Add the oil, egg, and vanilla and pulse the mixer on medium speed a few times to incorporate the ingredients.

5. In a small saucepan, melt the butter over medium-high heat. Cook, stirring, until the butter begins to bubble, 2–3 minutes. Stir carefully with a spatula for another 3–4 minutes or until the butter begins to froth and turn brown as the solids on the bottom of the pan also turn a rich deep brown and it smells nutty and fragrant.

6. Turn off the heat and immediately pour in the milk to stop the cooking process. Be careful of splatters and steam. Add the lemon juice and stir to combine.

7. Pour the milk mixture into the banana mixture, scraping the saucepan to get all the delicious nut-brown bits off the bottom. Pulse the mixer on medium speed a few times to combine.

continued →

8. Add the flour mixture to the banana mixture. Mix on low speed for 10–20 seconds, then turn the speed to medium and mix for another 10–20 seconds. The mixture should be combined and smooth, like a thick pancake batter. Scrape down the sides of the bowl while mixing so that you don't leave any unmixed bits at the bottom.

9. Remove the dulce de leche from the fridge and give it a good stir until it is slightly softened and smooth. Drizzle ¼ cup (60 ml) of the dulce de leche evenly over the muffin batter, and swirl it in gently, taking care not to overmix.

10. Divide the batter evenly among the prepared muffin cups, making sure each scoop gets a swirl of dulce de leche. Top each muffin with a slice of banana and sprinkle the remaining macadamia nuts on top.

11. Bake for 25–30 minutes or until the muffins have risen and a skewer inserted in the center of a muffin comes out clean. Let cool completely in the tin on a wire rack.

12. Before serving, smear a teaspoon or two of the remaining dulce de leche on top of each muffin and dust with icing sugar.

These muffins are best eaten fresh, but will keep in an airtight container in the fridge for up to 3 days or wrapped individually in the freezer for up to 1 month.

KITCHEN NOTES:

1. You can make the muffin batter 1-2 days ahead of time and keep it covered in the fridge until you are ready to bake. Let the batter warm to room temperature before adding the dulce de leche in step 9.

2. Chopped peanuts also work wonderfully instead of macadamias in this recipe. Try adding a few tablespoons of peanut butter in with the bananas.

Buttermilk Scones

5 cups (750 g) all-purpose flour

5 tsp (21 g) baking powder

1 tsp baking soda

1 tsp kosher salt

1¼ cups (270 g) cold unsalted butter, cut into ¼-inch (6 mm) cubes

2 cups (500 ml) whole milk

⅓ cup + 3 Tbsp (120 ml) whipping cream, divided

2 tsp fresh lemon juice

Scones vary by region, kitchen, and preference. Some are high and fluffy; some are denser, like a biscuit. How you make your scones is really a personal preference. These ones are more on the biscuit side, best eaten warm and fresh with creamy butter, clotted cream, and jam or fresh fruit, though they hold up just as well for a beautiful eggs benny! These are the scones I grew up on, and I have great memories of my paternal nana baking them when we stayed with her. They were her go-to with an afternoon cuppa and a wicked game of Scrabble.

1. Using a fine-mesh sieve, sift the flour, baking powder, baking soda, and salt into a large bowl. With a pastry cutter or a fork, cut in the butter until the mixture resembles coarse meal.

2. In a large measuring jug, stir together the milk, ⅓ cup + 1 tablespoon (90 ml) of the whipping cream, and the lemon juice. Pour the milk mixture into the flour mixture and mix with a fork until just combined. It is important not to overmix! The more you handle the dough, the less light and fluffy the scones will be. The mixture will be a bit sticky and lumpy, and you may feel like it's not mixed enough. (It is.)

3. Dump the mixture onto a lightly floured surface. Using your fingertips, gently pat (do not knead) the mixture into an 8 × 12-inch (20 × 30 cm) rectangle, about ¾ inch (2 cm) thick, making sure the dough is sticking together loosely. Sprinkle a bit of flour on the dough if it's sticking to your hands or the countertop.

4. Divide the dough in half and flip one half over the other. Gently press it down with your fingertips until it is about 1 inch (2.5 cm) thick and about 8 × 12 inches (20 × 30 cm) again.

5. Using a 3- to 4-inch (8–10 cm) cookie cutter or a thin-edged glass, cut as many rounds as you can, dipping the cutter in flour as needed to avoid sticking. Try not to twist the cutter, or the scones won't rise evenly. Gently gather the scraps together and cut more rounds. Place the scones on a pan or large plate, cover loosely with plastic wrap, and refrigerate for 1 hour.

6. Meanwhile, preheat the oven to 400°F (200°C). Line two large rimmed sheet pans with parchment paper.

7. Place six to eight scones on each pan, leaving as much room as possible between each, and brush with the remaining whipping cream.

8. Bake for 17–20 minutes or until the scones have risen and are light golden. Transfer the scones to a wire rack and let cool for 5 minutes. Serve warm.

These scones will keep in an airtight container at room temperature for up to 3 days or in the freezer for up to 1 month.

Blueberry Lemon Scones

5 cups (750 g) all-purpose flour

5 tsp (21 g) baking powder

1 tsp baking soda

1 tsp kosher salt

1¼ cups (270 g) cold unsalted butter, cut into ½-inch (1.2 cm) cubes

1½ cups (375 ml) whole milk

⅓ cup + 3 Tbsp (120 ml) whipping cream, divided

2 tsp finely grated lemon zest

2 Tbsp (30 ml) fresh lemon juice

½ cup (125 ml) Sprite, 7UP, or similar soft drink

1½ cups (190 g) frozen blueberries

1 Tbsp granulated sugar, for sprinkling

Lemon Curd (page 251; optional)

You may be surprised to find Sprite in this recipe! Years ago, my sous chef and good friend Chris told me about his grandmother's scone recipe, which contained the fizzy soft drink. My nana, who was also famous for her scones (see page 71), might roll over in her grave if she knew I was making scones with soda pop! As you can imagine, I was hesitant to include this ingredient, but it adds a unique sweet flavor, and the bubbles give the scones a bit of a lighter texture. This is a fun recipe to make with your kids, as they will be sure to find great joy in pouring soda into the bowl!

1. Using a fine-mesh sieve, sift the flour, baking powder, baking soda, and salt into a large bowl. With a pastry cutter or a fork, cut in the butter until the mixture resembles coarse meal.

2. In a large measuring jug, stir together the milk, ⅓ cup + 1 tablespoon (90 ml) of the whipping cream, and the lemon zest and lemon juice. Pour the milk mixture into the flour mixture, add the Sprite, and mix with a fork until just combined. It is important not to overmix! The more you handle the dough, the less light and fluffy the scones will be. The mixture will be sticky and lumpy, and you may feel like it's not mixed enough. (It is.)

3. Gently fold in the blueberries so they are evenly dispersed throughout the dough.

4. Dump the mixture onto a lightly floured surface. Using your fingertips, gently pat (do not knead) the mixture into an 8 × 12-inch (20 × 30 cm) rectangle, about ¾ inch (2 cm) thick, making sure the dough is sticking together loosely. Sprinkle a bit of flour on the dough if it's sticking to your hands or the countertop.

5. Divide the dough in half and flip one half over the other. Gently press it down with your fingertips until it is about 1 inch (2.5 cm) thick and about 8 × 12 inches (20 × 30 cm) again.

6. Using a large chef's knife, trim the edges of the dough to square it up. Cut it in half lengthwise, then cut each length into three even squares. Cut each square in half diagonally to create a triangle. Place the scones on a pan or large plate, cover loosely with plastic wrap, and refrigerate for 1 hour.

7. Meanwhile, preheat the oven to 400°F (200°C). Line two large rimmed sheet pans with parchment paper.

8. Place six scones on each pan, leaving as much room as possible between each. Brush with the remaining whipping cream and sprinkle the tops with sugar.

9. Bake for 20–25 minutes or until the scones have risen and are light golden. Transfer the scones to a wire rack and let cool for 5 minutes. Serve warm, with lemon curd, if desired.

   These scones will keep in an airtight container at room temperature for up to 2 days or in the freezer for up to 1 month.

Jalapeño Cheddar Scones

5 cups (750 g) all-purpose flour

5 tsp (21 g) baking powder

1 tsp baking soda

1 tsp kosher salt

1¼ cups (270 g) cold unsalted butter, cut into ¼-inch (6 mm) cubes

2 cups (500 ml) whole milk

⅓ cup + 3 Tbsp (120 ml) whipping cream, divided

2 tsp fresh lemon juice

2 cups (180 g) coarsely grated aged Cheddar cheese, divided

¼ cup (35 g) drained and roughly chopped pickled jalapeños

¼ cup (20 g) flat-leaf parsley, roughly chopped

⅓ cup (38 g) dry polenta or cornmeal, for topping (optional)

When I was running my restaurant Sage, my organic farmer brought me a feast of fresh jalapeño peppers. This recipe, along with several others, was born of the need to use up the many jars of pickled peppers we processed to preserve this unexpected bounty. The combination of the vinegary jalapeños and the sharp Cheddar gives these scones a unique and tangy bite.

1. Using a fine-mesh sieve, sift the flour, baking powder, baking soda, and salt into a large bowl. With a pastry cutter or a fork, cut in the butter until the mixture resembles coarse meal.

2. In a large measuring jug, stir together the milk, ⅓ cup + 1 tablespoon (90 ml) of the whipping cream, and the lemon juice. Pour the milk mixture into the flour mixture and mix with a fork until just combined. Don't overmix! The more you handle the dough, the less light and fluffy the scones will be. The mixture will be sticky and lumpy, and you may feel like it's not mixed enough. (It is.)

3. Gently mix in 1⅓ cups (120 g) of grated cheese and the jalapeños and parsley.

4. Dump the mixture onto a lightly floured surface (you can use polenta or cornmeal in place of flour, if desired). Using your fingertips, gently pat (do not knead) the mixture into an 8 × 12-inch (20 × 30 cm) rectangle, about ¾ inch (2 cm) thick, making sure the dough is sticking together loosely. Sprinkle a bit of flour on the dough if it's sticking to your hands or the countertop.

5. Divide the dough in half and flip one half onto the other. Gently press it down with your fingertips until it is about 1 inch (2.5 cm) thick and about 8 × 12 inches (20 × 30 cm) again.

6. Using a 3- to 4-inch (8–10 cm) cookie cutter or a thin-edged glass, cut as many rounds as you can, dipping the cutter in flour as needed to avoid sticking. Try not to twist the cutter, or the scones won't rise evenly. Gently gather the scraps together and cut more rounds. Place the scones on a pan or large plate, cover loosely with plastic wrap, and refrigerate for 1 hour.

7. Meanwhile, preheat the oven to 400°F (200°C). Line two large rimmed sheet pans with parchment paper.

8. Place six to eight scones on each pan, leaving as much room as possible between each (the cheese will cause them to spread a little). Brush with the remaining whipping cream. Sprinkle with the polenta (if using) and the remaining cheese.

9. Bake for 17–20 minutes or until the scones have risen and are light golden. Transfer the scones to a wire rack and let cool for 5 minutes. Serve warm.

These scones will keep in an airtight container at room temperature for up to 3 days or in the freezer for up to 1 month.

Cinnamon Honey Scones

5 cups (750 g) all-purpose
flour

5 tsp (21 g) baking powder

1 tsp baking soda

1 tsp kosher salt

1¼ cups (270 g) cold
unsalted butter, cut into
¼-inch (6 mm) cubes

2 cups (500 ml) whole milk

⅓ cup + 3 Tbsp (120 ml)
whipping cream, divided

2 tsp fresh lemon juice

1 Tbsp ground cinnamon,
plus 2 tsp for dusting

3 Tbsp (45 mL) good-quality
honey, divided

Making hundreds of scones commercially can leave you with a lot of scraps of dough. One day, we had a Crust team brainstorming session and came up with a multitude of ideas, deciding on several new sweet and savory scone flavors to try with our customers. When we presented these in the shop, they were immediately gobbled up. They make the house smell amazing while baking and are excellent for taking over as a greeting to a new neighbor. They're so good, they might be polished off right out of the oven, so feel free to double this recipe.

1. Using a fine-mesh sieve, sift the flour, baking powder, baking soda, and salt into a large bowl. With a pastry cutter or a fork, cut in the butter until the mixture resembles coarse meal.

2. In a large measuring jug, stir together the milk, ⅓ cup + 1 tablespoon (90 ml) of the whipping cream, and the lemon juice. Pour the milk mixture into the flour mixture and mix with a fork until just combined. It is important not to overmix! The more you handle the dough, the less light and fluffy the scones will be. The mixture will be a bit sticky and lumpy, and you may feel like it's not mixed enough. (It is.)

3. Add 1 tablespoon of cinnamon and 2 tablespoons (30 ml) of honey. Lightly swirl through the mixture. It will be messy and sticky, but it will be worth it.

4. Dump the mixture out onto a lightly floured surface. Using your fingertips, gently pat (do not knead) the mixture into a 12-inch (30 cm) square, about ¾ inch (2 cm) thick, making sure the dough is sticking together loosely. Sprinkle a bit of flour on the dough if it's sticking to your hands or the countertop.

5. Divide the dough in half and flip one half onto the other. Gently press it down with your fingertips until it is about 1 inch (2.5 cm) thick and 12 inches (30 cm) square.

6. Using a sharp knife, trim the edges and cut into twelve equal pieces. Place the scones on a pan or large plate, cover loosely with plastic wrap, and refrigerate for 1 hour.

7. Meanwhile, preheat the oven to 400°F (200°C). Line two large rimmed sheet pans with parchment paper.

8. Place six scones on each pan, leaving as much room as possible between each, and brush with the remaining whipping cream. Drizzle with the remaining honey and dust with the remaining cinnamon.

9. Bake for 17–20 minutes or until the scones have risen and are light golden. Transfer the scones to a wire rack and let cool for 5 minutes. Serve warm.

   These scones will keep in an airtight container at room temperature for up to 3 days or in the freezer for up to 1 month.

KITCHEN NOTES:

1. You can wrap the biscuits tightly in plastic wrap and freeze them before they are baked. They will keep in the freezer for about 2 weeks. Thaw in the fridge before baking.

2. Reese taught me that it's important not to twist the cutter when you are cutting biscuits. Hang onto the cutter firmly and simply press straight down; otherwise, your biscuits will rise and bake a little crooked and twisty.

Reese's Chorizo Biscuits

2 Tbsp (30 ml) extra virgin olive oil

½ white onion, cut into ½-inch (1.2 cm) dice

3.3 oz (100 g) link smoked chorizo, cut into ¼-inch (6 mm) dice

¼ cup (20 g) roughly chopped flat-leaf parsley

1 tsp finely grated lemon zest

1 tsp mild smoked paprika

1¼ tsp kosher salt, divided

½ tsp freshly cracked black pepper

5 cups (750 g) all-purpose flour, plus more for sprinkling

5 tsp (21 g) baking powder

1 tsp baking soda

1¼ cups (270 g) cold unsalted butter, cut into ¼-inch (6 mm) cubes

2 cups (500 ml) whole milk

8 Tbsp (120 ml) whipping cream, divided

2 tsp fresh lemon juice

1 cup (90 g) grated smoked Cheddar or Gouda cheese, divided

I affectionately named these after a longtime employee and mate here at Crust, who would ask me at least once a week to add some crumbled chorizo to our buttermilk biscuits. I put it off for years. Now, of course, I regret waiting so long! These biscuits are fantastic. Reese was the one who taught me that the secret to a fabulous biscuit is to handle the dough as little as possible. It will be crumbly and messy, and you may wonder if the biscuits will work out. (Spoiler—they do. Brilliantly.)

1. In a small sauté pan over low heat, heat the oil. Add the onion and chorizo and cook slowly and gently, stirring often, until the onion is lightly caramelized, about 10 minutes. Remove from the heat and stir in the parsley, lemon zest, paprika, ¼ teaspoon of salt, and the pepper. Let cool completely.

2. Using a fine-mesh sieve, sift the flour, baking powder, baking soda, and remaining salt into a large bowl. With a pastry cutter or a fork, cut in the butter until the mixture resembles coarse meal.

3. In a large measuring jug, stir together the milk, 6 tablespoons (90 ml) of the whipping cream, and the lemon juice. Pour the milk mixture into the flour mixture and mix with a fork until the dough is just combined and still crumbly. The dough won't come together yet and may not feel like it's mixed enough. (It is.)

4. Gently fold the chorizo mixture and about ⅔ cup (60 g) of the cheese into the dough until just combined.

5. Dump the mixture onto a lightly floured surface. Scoop it together with your hands, then very lightly knead the mixture until it has just barely come together enough that it is not falling apart. Sprinkle about a teaspoon of flour on top of the dough, then pat it gently into a round about ¾ inch (2 cm) thick.

6. Using a 3- to 4-inch (8–10 cm) cookie cutter or a thin-edged glass, cut as many rounds as you can and place them on a large plate. It's okay if they overlap. Gently gather the scraps of dough together and cut more rounds. Add them to the plate. Cover the biscuits loosely with plastic wrap and refrigerate for 1 hour.

7. Meanwhile, preheat the oven to 400°F (200°C). Line a large rimmed sheet pan with parchment paper.

8. Place six to eight biscuits on the pan and brush with a bit of whipping cream. Sprinkle with half of the remaining cheese. Leave the rest of the biscuits in the fridge until ready to bake.

9. Bake for 17–20 minutes or until the biscuits have risen and are light golden. Transfer the biscuits to a wire rack and let cool for 5 minutes. Serve warm. Repeat steps 8 and 9 with the remaining biscuits.

These biscuits will keep in an airtight container at room temperature for up to 3 days or in the freezer for up to 1 month.

Abby's Favorite Chocolate Rice Krispie Squares

MAKES 16 SQUARES

¼ cup (60 g) unsalted butter

1 package (8 oz/250 g) large white marshmallows

½ cup (90 g) semisweet dark chocolate chips, divided

½ cup (50 g) cocoa powder

½ tsp pure vanilla extract

5 cups (150 g) puffed rice cereal, such as Rice Krispies

Having watched her dad cook and bake her whole life, it was inevitable that my daughter, Abby, would have the same culinary tendencies. She definitely inherited my sweet tooth, and these simple treats were the first things she invented on her own. This wasn't something we ever made in Australia; the humble Rice Krispie square seems to be purely North American. Abby took them to the next level with a bit of chocolate, and sometimes she adds a few sprinkles or candies on top. I've tried to add healthy ingredients like granola and hemp hearts to the mix, but my savvy children pick up on the difference immediately. Suffice it to say that I've only been able to get away with that once!

1. Grease an 8-inch (20 cm) square × 2-inch (5 cm) deep baking pan.

2. In a large saucepan over medium heat, melt the butter until it starts to bubble. Turn off the heat and stir in the marshmallows and half of the chocolate chips. Cover with a tight-fitting lid and leave for 2 minutes.

3. Sift the cocoa into the pot. Add the vanilla. Stir well, until all the ingredients are combined. With a large spoon, stir in the cereal. Work quickly so the mixture doesn't seize as it cools, but be careful, as the marshmallows will be very hot!

4. Spread the cereal mixture evenly in the prepared pan. Immediately top with the remaining chocolate chips. The residual heat of the marshmallows should melt them a little.

5. Let set for at least 1 hour at room temperature, then cut the slab into sixteen pieces.

These things don't last very long in our house, but we store them in an airtight container at room temperature for up to a week. I wouldn't suggest storing them in the fridge or freezer.

Not Pennye's Brownies

1¼ cups (187 g)
all-purpose flour

⅓ cup (35 g) cocoa powder

1 tsp baking powder

½ tsp kosher salt

3 eggs

¾ cup + 2 Tbsp (175 g)
granulated sugar

1 tsp pure vanilla extract

¾ cup (175 g) unsalted
butter

2 cups (360 g) semisweet
dark chocolate chips

1 cup (140 g) chopped
walnuts

These brownies are aptly named. One day my wife, Pennye, decided to make brownies, and the recipe called for 4 ounces of chocolate. When I happened upon her in the kitchen as she was embarking on her brownie-making adventure, she asked me how to measure the chocolate in ounces. When I explained that she would have to pull out the scale, she looked at me and very earnestly asked if we couldn't just measure it with the one-ounce jigger, as we would bourbon or gin. It took me a minute to decide if she was joking (she wasn't). I won't tell you how those brownies turned out, but I will tell you that these are not them.

1. Preheat the oven to 350°F (180°C). Grease an 8 × 12-inch (20 × 30 cm) baking pan and line it with parchment paper.

2. Using a fine-mesh sieve, sift the flour, cocoa, baking powder, and salt into a bowl.

3. In a stand mixer, combine the eggs, sugar, and vanilla. Using the whisk attachment, whip on high speed until the mixture is pale, fluffy, and roughly doubled in volume, about 4 minutes.

4. Meanwhile, in a medium saucepan over medium heat, melt the butter and heat until bubbling, about 4 minutes. Remove from the heat and add the chocolate chips. Cover with a tight-fitting lid and leave for 2–3 minutes, then whisk until the chocolate has melted and is completely smooth.

5. With the mixer on low speed, slowly drizzle the chocolate into the egg mixture. Increase the speed to medium and mix until completely combined, 30–45 seconds.

6. Remove the bowl from the stand and, using a wide spatula, fold in the flour mixture until completely combined. Fold in the walnuts. Mix thoroughly, ensuring there are no pockets of unmixed flour. Gently fold in any you missed.

7. Pour the batter into the prepared pan and smooth the top gently with a spatula.

8. Bake for 18–24 minutes or until the brownies have risen in the middle and started to crack around the edges, but seem a little underdone if tested with a skewer. Let cool in the pan on a wire rack for about 30 minutes, to give it time to set, before cutting into squares.

These brownies will keep in an airtight container at room temperature for up to 3 days or in the fridge for up to 2 weeks, or individually wrapped with plastic in the freezer for up to 1 month (I occasionally put them in my kids' lunches, and they are thawed by snack time).

Cakes

"To be loved. To be desired.
Like the raspberry pastries
in the bakery window."

CAMILLA GREBE

KITCHEN NOTES:

1. Make sure to cook this batter immediately. The salt draws out moisture from the zucchini, and if it is not baked right away, it tends to turn into a wet, sloppy mess!

2. This batter can also be used to make individual tea cakes if you have such pans in your cupboard. Simply reduce the baking time to 25-35 minutes, depending on the size. Test with a skewer for doneness.

Zucchini Marmalade Cake

1½ cups + 2 Tbsp (240 g)
all-purpose flour

3 tsp ground cinnamon,
divided

½ tsp baking soda

½ tsp baking powder

½ tsp kosher salt

2 eggs, at room temperature

1 cup (200 g) granulated
sugar, divided

½ cup (125 ml) vegetable oil

⅓ cup (120 g) orange
marmalade

1½ cups (250 g) coarsely
grated zucchini (about
1 large)

1 cup (140 g) toasted
walnut halves, roughly
chopped

When I was a kid, we had one young orange tree in the backyard. The tree didn't produce much fruit, so our mum would claim all of it to use for marmalade. We would get into a lot of trouble if we picked any, though truth be told, they did make great projectiles! The fruit was quite tart, and perfect for marmalade, but not great for eating straight off the tree. Now, years later, each time I make orange marmalade I am launched back to those cold winter days when Mum would have it bubbling away on the stove. She was constantly trying to sneak vegetables into all of our cakes and snacks, and this cake is a perfect example of that! This recipe is such a nice combination of winter preserves and fresh summer harvest.

---

1. Preheat the oven to 350°F (180°C). Spray or brush an 8½ × 4½-inch (22 × 11 cm) loaf pan with a neutral oil, then carefully line it with parchment paper, cutting pieces to fit so they tuck nicely into the corners.

2. Using a fine-mesh sieve, sift the flour, 1 teaspoon of the cinnamon, and the baking soda, baking powder, and salt into a medium bowl.

3. In a stand mixer, combine the eggs, ¾ cup (150 g) of the sugar, and the oil and marmalade. Using the paddle attachment, mix on low speed until combined, 20–30 seconds. Scrape down the sides of the bowl with a spatula to ensure everything has been incorporated. Add the zucchini and mix for a few seconds until combined.

4. Carefully add the flour mixture and mix on low speed until just combined, 20–30 seconds. Using a spatula, scrape down the bowl to ensure everything has been incorporated.

5. Remove the bowl from the mixer and gently fold in the walnuts.

6. Pour the batter into the prepared pan and gently smooth the top with your spatula.

7. In a small mixing bowl, combine the remaining ¼ cup (50 g) granulated sugar and the remaining 2 teaspoons cinnamon. Sprinkle over the top of the loaf.

8. Bake for 50–60 minutes or until the cake is a deep golden brown and a skewer inserted in the center comes out clean. Let cool in the pan on a wire rack for about 10–15 minutes.

9. Invert the loaf onto the wire rack, remove the pan, then tip the loaf right side up. Let cool completely before serving. (I love it slathered with salted butter and a bit more marmalade.)

This cake will keep in an airtight container in the fridge for up to 5 days. It doesn't freeze well, as the zucchini turns into an unappetizing texture.

Chocolate Sour Cream and Raspberry Cake

½ cup (90 g) semisweet dark chocolate chips

⅔ cup (100 g) all-purpose flour

½ cup (50 g) cocoa powder

1 tsp baking powder

¾ cup + 1 Tbsp + 2 tsp (100 g) almond flour, lightly packed

¼ tsp kosher salt

1¼ cups (250 g) granulated sugar

4 eggs

1 cup (250 ml) vegetable oil

½ cup (125 ml) full-fat sour cream

1 tsp pure vanilla extract

1 cup (130 g) raspberries

2 Tbsp (25 g) coarse sugar

To Garnish

1 cup (130 g) raspberries

1 cup (250 ml) Dark Chocolate Ganache (page 244), melted

1 Tbsp roughly chopped toasted almonds (optional)

At Crust, we serve this recipe as individual cakes. They haven't always been quite like this, though; they started out as simple chocolate tea cakes and have evolved over the years into the decadent dessert they are today. First, we added sour cream for moistness and richness. Then we replaced most of the all-purpose flour with almond flour, giving it a bit more of a pleasantly dense texture. The raspberries came next, followed by a chocolate drizzle (why not?), and, lastly, needing a bit of a crunch, we sprinkled them with chopped toasted almonds. I bring this to you here in loaf form, which makes a lovely presentation at teatime or for dessert.

1. Preheat the oven to 325°F (160°C). Line an 8½ × 4½-inch (22 × 11 cm) loaf pan with parchment paper, cutting pieces to fit so they tuck nicely into the corners.

2. Bring a medium pot with about 1 inch (2.5 cm) of water to a boil, then lower the heat to a simmer. Top with a stainless steel bowl that is just big enough to fit snugly on top of the pot without touching the water. Add the chocolate chips and stir gently with a spatula until silky smooth. (Alternatively, you can microwave the chocolate in a bowl for 20 seconds at a time, stirring well after each interval, for about 1 minute, until melted and smooth. With either method, be careful not to overheat it, or the chocolate will seize and won't be usable.)

3. Using a fine-mesh sieve, sift the all-purpose flour, cocoa, and baking powder into a stand mixer bowl. Add the almond flour and salt.

4. In a large measuring jug or bowl, whisk together the granulated sugar, eggs, oil, sour cream, and vanilla. An immersion blender will work best here, but if you don't have one, a wire whisk and some elbow grease will do. Add the melted chocolate, starting with a tablespoon or two, then slowly drizzle in the remainder. Blend well, until well emulsified.

5. Pour the chocolate mixture into the flour mixture and, using the paddle attachment on medium-low, mix gently to just combine all the ingredients, about 30 seconds. Be careful not to overmix. Using a spatula, fold in the raspberries and ensure all ingredients are mixed in properly.

6. Pour the batter into the prepared pan and gently smooth the top with a small spatula. Sprinkle the coarse sugar evenly on top.

continued →

7. Bake for 60 minutes. Cover the loaf with foil, rotate it halfway, and bake for 45 minutes or until a skewer inserted in the center comes out clean. Let cool in the pan on a wire rack for about 15 minutes.

8. Invert the loaf onto the wire rack, remove the pan, then tip the loaf right side up. Let cool completely. Serve garnished with raspberries, chocolate ganache, and almonds (if using).

This cake will keep in an airtight container at room temperature for up to 3 days or in the fridge for up to 1 week. I like to individually wrap and freeze 1-inch (2.5 cm) slices (without the berries, chocolate, and nuts on top). They will keep for about 1 month.

KITCHEN NOTES:

1. If the ganache needs remelting, see note on page 245.

2. For a twist on this cake, smear Nutella on top and sprinkle with plenty of crushed toasted hazelnuts before serving.

Pumpkin and Ginger Teacake

with Bourbon Maple Glaze

SERVES 8

Pumpkin Seed Praline

¼ cup (35 g) unsalted raw pumpkin seeds

¼ cup (35 g) chopped raw walnuts

2 tsp light brown sugar, lightly packed

1 tsp light corn syrup

½ tsp maple syrup

¼ tsp kosher salt

⅛ tsp cayenne pepper

2 Tbsp (25 g) finely chopped candied ginger

Teacake

2 eggs

⅓ cup (75 ml) vegetable oil

1 cup (250 ml) pure pumpkin purée (see note)

1⅓ cups (200 g) all-purpose flour

1 cup (200 g) granulated sugar

1 tsp baking soda

1 tsp baking powder

1 tsp ground allspice

1 tsp ground cinnamon

1 tsp ground ginger

½ tsp ground cloves

¼ tsp kosher salt

⅓ cup (50 g) roughly chopped candied ginger, roughly chopped

Pumpkin isn't a huge staple of autumn in Australia, but, as we all know, it is in North America. I wanted to create something for the bakery that included the traditional flavor of pumpkin, but also wanted to directly honor my newly laid roots in Canada—hence the maple glaze. This cake is the perfect accompaniment to warming by the fire, alone with a book or with friends and conversation, an excellent vanilla ice cream and a bit of extra maple syrup on the side. The scent of it baking will warm the house and your spirits in equal measure.

1. **MAKE THE PRALINE:** Preheat the oven to 350°F (180°C). Line a large rimmed sheet pan with parchment paper.

2. Directly on the sheet pan, combine the pumpkin seeds, walnuts, brown sugar, corn syrup, maple syrup, salt, and cayenne. Mix thoroughly.

3. Bake for 7 minutes, then give everything a stir. Bake for another 5–10 minutes or until the sugar melts and begins to get sticky and the nuts are a little browned.

4. Give the mixture another stir and spread it out evenly. Let cool completely, then add the ginger, stirring well to incorporate all the pieces. (If making ahead, the praline can be stored in an airtight plastic bag at room temperature for up to 2 weeks.)

5. **MAKE THE TEACAKE:** Spray an 8½ × 4½-inch (22 × 11 cm) loaf pan with a neutral oil and carefully line it with parchment paper, cutting pieces to fit so they tuck nicely into the corners.

6. In a medium bowl, whisk together the eggs and oil. Add the pumpkin purée and stir well.

7. In another medium bowl, whisk together the flour, granulated sugar, baking soda, baking powder, allspice, cinnamon, ground ginger, cloves, and salt.

8. Using a large spatula, fold the flour mixture into the pumpkin mixture until just combined. Gently fold in the candied ginger.

9. Pour the batter into the prepared pan and gently smooth the top with a small spatula.

10. Bake for 40–50 minutes or until the loaf has risen and is golden brown on top, and a skewer inserted in the center comes out clean.

continued →

Bourbon Maple Glaze

¼ cup (60 ml) maple syrup

2 Tbsp (30 ml) water

1 Tbsp good-quality dark bourbon (optional, see note)

To Assemble

1 Tbsp clear corn syrup

1 Tbsp icing sugar

11. **MAKE THE GLAZE:** Meanwhile, stir together the maple syrup, water, and bourbon (if using) in a small measuring jug.

12. **ASSEMBLE THE CAKE:** As soon as the cake comes out of the oven, carefully pour the syrup over the loaf and let it absorb. Let cool completely in the pan on a wire rack, then carefully remove the cake from the pan and place it on a serving platter.

13. Brush the top of the loaf with corn syrup. Sprinkle the praline on top, patting it down gently to ensure it sticks. Dust with icing sugar, then slice to serve.

This cake will keep in an airtight container at room temperature for up to 3 days or in the freezer for up to 1 month.

KITCHEN NOTES:

1. Cooked and puréed butternut squash is an excellent replacement for the pumpkin purée.

2. If you prefer not to use bourbon, simply omit it. The cake will be just as tasty.

Mr. Rich Birthday Cake

Mousse Filling

1½ cups (265 g) semisweet dark chocolate chips

2 cups (500 ml) whipping cream, divided

2 Tbsp (16 g) icing sugar

1 tsp pure vanilla extract

Cakes

1½ cups (225 g) all-purpose flour

1½ cups (200 g) cake or pastry flour (see page 12)

1 tsp baking soda

1 tsp baking powder

1 tsp kosher salt

1 cup (100 g) cocoa powder, sifted

1½ cups (300 g) granulated sugar

1½ cups (375 ml) hot water

1 cup (250 ml) vegetable oil

½ cup (125 ml) whole milk

2 tsp fresh lemon juice

1 tsp pure vanilla extract

3 eggs, at room temperature

Chocolate Pecan Streusel

½ cup (75 g) all-purpose flour

½ cup (70 g) finely chopped raw pecans

⅓ cup (67 g) light brown sugar, lightly packed

¼ cup (25 g) cocoa powder, sifted

¼ cup (60 g) unsalted

This cake has been around at Crust for many years. I can't really remember where the name came from, though I do have a vague recollection of it coming to life around the height of the hit show *Sex and the City*, which featured a love interest named Mr. Big. (My wife was, ahem, a big fan.) I suppose the show was on in the background while I made a cake for a friend's birthday party, and his name was swirling around in my head as I tasted the first bite, thereby christening it Mr. Rich. This cake is aptly named: dark, chocolatey, and rich. It's suitable for birthday parties and viewing parties alike.

1. **MAKE THE FILLING:** Place the chocolate chips in a heatproof mixing bowl. In a small pot, bring 1 cup (250 ml) of the whipping cream to a rapid boil and immediately pour over the chocolate. Gently whisk until the chocolate is completely melted. Let cool for 10 minutes.

2. Meanwhile, pour the remaining 1 cup (250 ml) whipping cream into a stand mixer bowl and add the icing sugar and vanilla. Using the whisk attachment, whip until the cream forms medium peaks.

3. Spoon about one-third of the whipped cream into the chocolate ganache and gently stir through to help cool down the ganache. When it is just combined, add another third of the cream and stir until barely combined.

4. Pour the chocolate mixture into the remaining whipped cream and fold with a spatula until barely combined. Try not to overmix, and don't worry about a few cream streaks. Transfer to a clean container, cover, and refrigerate for at least 2–3 hours or until needed, up to 2 days.

5. **MAKE THE CAKES:** Preheat the oven to 350°F (180°C). Spray or brush two 9-inch (23 cm) round cake pans with a neutral oil and line the bottoms with parchment paper.

6. Using a fine-mesh sieve, sift the all-purpose flour, pastry flour, baking soda, baking powder, and salt into a medium bowl.

7. In a large bowl, sift the cocoa then add the granulated sugar. Carefully pour in the hot water and whisk together for about 15 seconds or until there are no lumps. Add the oil, milk, lemon juice, and vanilla, and continue whisking until well combined. Add the eggs and whisk until incorporated.

8. Fold in the flour mixture until just combined. Using a spatula, scrape the sides and bottom of the bowl to ensure everything has been incorporated.

9. Pour the batter into the prepared pans and gently smooth the tops with the spatula.

continued →

butter, softened

½ tsp baking powder

¼ tsp kosher salt

<u>To Assemble</u>

1½ cups (190 g) fresh
or frozen raspberries

Cocoa powder, for dusting

KITCHEN NOTE:

1. You can find special
   knives and measuring tools
   that help to slice a cake
   crosswise with razor-sharp
   accuracy. You can also
   measure and mark the cake
   with toothpicks or wrap a
   bit of kitchen twine around
   the cake to mark the spot
   to start slicing. The last
   thing you want after baking
   such a beauty is to slice
   it all off-balance!

10. Bake for 35–40 minutes, swapping and rotating the pans after about 20 minutes for even baking, until the cakes have risen evenly and a skewer inserted in the center of a cake comes out clean. Let cool in the pans on a wire rack for 10–15 minutes, then carefully transfer the cakes to the rack to cool completely, at least 1 hour.

11. **MAKE THE STREUSEL:** Preheat the oven to 350°F (180°C) and line a rimmed sheet pan with parchment paper.

12. In a medium bowl, combine the flour, pecans, brown sugar, cocoa, butter, baking powder, and salt. Using your fingertips, mix until it's crumbly and lumpy.

13. Sprinkle the crumble evenly onto the prepared pan, crumbling it through your fingertips to create small lumps of streusel no bigger than a peanut. Refrigerate for 10 minutes.

14. Bake the streusel for 8 minutes, then give it a stir to break up the lumps. Bake for another 5–10 minutes or until the streusel is cooked through and the pecans start to turn golden brown. (It tastes better a little undercooked than overcooked.) Let cool on the pan for at least 1 hour before using. (Store in an airtight container at room temperature for up to 2 days if you are not using it right away. Be sure to let it cool completely so it doesn't lose its crispness.)

15. **ASSEMBLE THE CAKE:** Using a serrated bread knife, trim off the top of each cooled cake so that it is 1 inch (2.5 cm) high. Cut each cake in half crosswise, giving you four layers, each ½ inch (1.2 cm) high and flat on the top and bottom (see note).

16. Starting with a cake layer with an uncut bottom, place it cut side up on a serving plate or cake stand. (Save the other round with an uncut bottom for the final layer; it's easier to frost and gives an even look to your finished cake.) Using a small offset spatula, spread one-quarter of the chocolate mousse evenly over top. Sprinkle one-third of the raspberries evenly over the mousse, tearing up a few to vary the look of the berries.

17. Press a second cake layer firmly on top of the first, making sure it is level and flat. Spread another quarter of the mousse on top, then sprinkle with another third of the raspberries. Repeat with a third cake layer, another quarter of the mousse, and the remaining raspberries. Place the final layer cut side down. Carefully wrap the cake with plastic wrap and chill in the fridge for at least 1 hour or overnight.

18. Spread the remaining mousse on top of the cake and sprinkle the streusel over the mousse. Finish with a light dusting of cocoa. Serve cold.

    This cake will keep in an airtight container in the fridge for up to 3 days. I don't recommend freezing it.

Sticky Toffee Date Cake

SERVES 10–12

Cake

2 cups (300 g) seedless dried dates (see note)

1 tsp baking soda

1⅔ cups (400 ml) boiling water

2 cups (300 g) all-purpose flour

2 tsp baking powder

½ tsp kosher salt

6 Tbsp (90 g) unsalted butter, at room temperature, cut into ½-inch (1.2 cm) pieces

¾ cup (150 g) light brown sugar, lightly packed

3 eggs, at room temperature, lightly beaten

2 tsp pure vanilla extract

Toffee Sauce

½ cup (115 g) unsalted butter

1 cup (200 g) dark brown sugar, lightly packed

2 tsp flaky sea salt (see note)

1 cup (250 ml) whipping cream

2 Tbsp (30 ml) bourbon (optional)

2 tsp pure vanilla extract

To Garnish

Whipped cream or clotted cream

Sticky toffee date cake, also known as sticky toffee pudding, is one of those Australian staples that can be found in bakeries, coffee shops, and cafés all over the country. Those who are not familiar with or particularly fond of dates may not be drawn to this cake, but don't let them scare you off. The dates add a beautiful chewiness and subtle sweetness to the cake, and if you didn't know they were part of the recipe, you might not even notice them! Served cold, warm, or at room temperature, the cake is wonderful on its own. The sauce is also lovely drizzled over vanilla ice cream.

1. **MAKE THE CAKE:** Preheat the oven to 350°F (180°C). Spray or brush a 10-inch (25 cm) Bundt pan with a neutral oil and place it on a parchment-lined large rimmed sheet pan.

2. Put the dates into a heatproof bowl. Sprinkle with the baking soda and pour the boiling water over top. Cover with plastic wrap and leave at room temperature for 10 minutes.

3. Meanwhile, using a fine-mesh sieve, sift the flour, baking powder, and salt into a medium bowl.

4. Add the butter to the date mixture and give it a quick stir. Transfer about ½ cup (125 ml) of the date mixture to a food processor and, using the S-shaped blade, pulse 8–10 times or until the dates are mashed up but still have a little texture. Scrape into a stand mixer bowl. Repeat with the remaining dates, ½ cup (125 ml) at a time, until they are all mashed.

5. Add the light brown sugar, eggs, and vanilla to the mixer bowl. Using the paddle attachment, mix on medium-low speed until combined, about 15 seconds. Add the date mixture and continue to mix for another 15 seconds.

6. Add the flour mixture and mix on low speed for 10 seconds to blend without it going everywhere! Turn the mixer to medium-high and mix for another 10–15 seconds or until it is completely combined and there are no lumps of flour left.

7. Pour the batter into the prepared Bundt pan and gently smooth the top with a spatula.

8. Bake for 40–45 minutes or until a skewer inserted in the center comes out clean. Let cool in the pan on a wire rack for about 20 minutes, then carefully turn it out onto the rack to cool.

continued →

9. **MAKE THE SAUCE:** In a small pot over medium heat, melt the butter. Add the dark brown sugar, salt, and whipping cream and stir with a spatula until well blended. Bring to a boil, scraping down the sides occasionally, then lower the heat to medium-low and simmer for about 3 minutes or it coats the back of a spoon. Toffee sauce thickens as it cools, so don't overcook it. Remove from the heat and stir in the bourbon (if using) and vanilla. (If making ahead, pour the sauce into a jar while still hot. Let cool, then cover and refrigerate for up to 2 weeks. Bring to room temperature before using.)

10. Cut the cake while it is still warm and serve with warm toffee sauce poured over each slice. Top with whipped or clotted cream as desired.

This cake will keep in an airtight container at room temperature for about 3 days, in the fridge for up to 1 week, or in the freezer for up to 1 month.

KITCHEN NOTES:

1. Feel each date for a seed and discard any you find. Even seedless dates sometimes have seeds!

2. Flaky sea salt is important here, for the flavor and for the measurement. If you only have kosher salt, cut it to ½ teaspoon.

3. To take this recipe to the next chocolatey level, replace ⅓ cup (50 g) of the all-purpose flour with ⅓ cup (35 g) of cocoa powder. Stir 2 tablespoons (22 g) dark chocolate chips into the hot toffee sauce.

4. If you want to make this cake in advance, let it cool completely and refrigerate the toffee sauce until set, about 2 hours. Using a small pallet knife, smear the cold sauce, which will have the consistency of frosting, all over the cake.

Angel Food Cake
with Raspberry Fool

Angel Food Cake

1¼ cups (160 g) cake or pastry flour (see page 12)

1¼ cups (300 ml) egg whites (about 10), at room temperature (see notes)

1½ tsp cream of tartar

½ tsp kosher salt

1½ cups (340 g) superfine sugar (see note)

1½ tsp pure vanilla extract

Raspberry Fool

2 cups (250 g) fresh or thawed frozen raspberries

¼ cup (50 g) granulated sugar

2 Tbsp (30 ml) raspberry liqueur, such as Chambord

2 cups (500 ml) whipping cream

½ cup (65 g) icing sugar

1 tsp pure vanilla extract

To Garnish

2 cups (250 g) fresh raspberries

⅓ cup (40 g) toasted pistachios, roughly chopped

Angel food cake is the blank canvas of baking and a great recipe to have in your repertoire. It is a fairly simple cake, not too sweet, and can be adorned any way you like. The fluffy, light crumb melts nicely in your mouth, and grabbing a slab for an afternoon snack is sometimes completely warranted! The raspberry fool (as strangely named as it is) also makes a dessert that stands on its own. While you can pair angel food cake with a huge variety of toppings, raspberry fool is a lovely option and is more elevated than plain whipped cream.

1. **MAKE THE CAKE:** Preheat the oven to 350°F (180°C). Have a 10-inch (25 cm) angel food cake pan ready, but do not grease it (see note).

2. Using a fine-mesh sieve, sift the flour into a medium bowl. Sift two more times to aerate it really well.

3. In a stand mixer, combine the egg whites, cream of tartar, and salt. Using the whisk attachment, mix on high speed for about 10 seconds to froth the whites slightly. (If you don't have a stand mixer, you can use a hand mixer.) While whisking, add the superfine sugar 1 tablespoon at a time. Whisk on high speed until the mixture forms soft peaks, about 2 minutes (see note).

4. Gently fold the flour into the egg whites until just combined. Be careful not to overmix, or you will lose too much volume and the cake will not be as light and fluffy. Using a spatula, scrape down the bowl so everything is incorporated.

5. Using a large spoon or ladle, spoon the batter into the cake pan. Lightly jiggle the pan (not tap it) to flatten out the top.

6. Lower the oven temperature to 325°F (160°C). Bake for 40–45 minutes or until a skewer inserted in the center comes out clean. (Don't be tempted to check on it for at least the first 30 minutes.) Turn the cake upside down onto a wire rack, but don't remove the pan. Let cool for 45–60 minutes. Run a small, thin knife around the edges of the pan to release the cake, remove the pan, and let cool completely on the rack.

7. **MAKE THE FOOL:** In a small mixing bowl, stir together the raspberries, granulated sugar, and raspberry liqueur. Let macerate for 10 minutes.

8. In the stand mixer, combine the whipping cream, icing sugar, and vanilla. Using the whisk attachment, whip on high speed until the cream forms soft peaks, 3–5 minutes. (If you don't have a stand mixer, you can use a hand mixer.)

continued →

9. Mash the raspberries completely, incorporating any liquid that has pooled in the bowl. Pour the raspberries into the whipped cream and stir once or twice with a spatula, swirling the raspberry purée through the cream and leaving decorative streaks. Be careful not to overmix, or the cream may curdle.

10. Spread the fool over the top and sides of the cake. Top with raspberries and sprinkle with pistachios. Serve immediately.

Before adding the raspberry fool, this cake will keep, wrapped well, at room temperature for 1–2 days or in the fridge for up to 1 week.

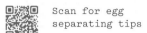 Scan for egg separating tips

---

KITCHEN NOTES:

1. Make sure your egg whites are absolutely yolk-free! Separate the eggs one at a time in case any yolks break. Scan the QR code to see how.

2. If you don't have superfine sugar, you can make it yourself quite easily. Place granulated sugar in a food processor or blender and whizz it until the sugar is superfine, 15-30 seconds.

3. Older eggs tend to be best for whisking, as they absorb more air when whisked. Don't whisk them too much—only to the soft peak stage, which means they don't hold a peak when you pull the whisk out of the bowl.

4. It is really important that all of your equipment is very clean and grease-free. As the cake bakes, the batter needs to grab on to the sides of the pan to help it rise and keep its structure; any grease on the pan will prevent that from happening. Grease will also prevent the egg whites from whipping up properly.

5. Make the raspberry fool only when you are ready to serve the cake. The whipped cream holds for 24 hours, but will start to collapse after that.

Lemon Curd
Poppy Seed Syrup Cakes

MAKES 12 INDIVIDUAL CAKES

Cakes

1 cup (200 g) granulated sugar

⅔ cup (150 ml) full-fat unsweetened plain Greek yogurt

⅔ cup (150 ml) vegetable oil

1 Tbsp finely grated lemon zest

½ cup (125 ml) fresh lemon juice

2 egg whites

1 tsp pure vanilla extract

¼ tsp kosher salt

1⅓ cups (200 g) all-purpose flour

2 tsp baking powder

2 Tbsp (20 g) poppy seeds

Lemon Syrup

⅔ cup (130 g) granulated sugar

½ cup (125 ml) light corn syrup

⅓ cup (75 ml) water

1 Tbsp finely grated lemon zest

¼ cup (60 ml) fresh lemon juice

I love keeping my Crust staff on their toes. Every once in a while, I call a team meeting to hash out new ideas, talk about our inspirations and thoughts on food trends, and share what we've spotted out there in the world. Together, we inevitably come up with a few new and exciting things to serve our customers. This is one of my great joys in life: seeing the enthusiasm and sparkly eyes around the kitchen as we use our palates, imaginations, and skills to join forces and create. This recipe was born of just such a collaboration! One suggestion layered with another, topped with yet another, and voila—we had a keeper.

1. **MAKE THE CAKES:** Preheat the oven to 350°F (180°C). Lightly spray or brush two 6-cup muffin trays (see note) with a neutral oil. Place the trays on a parchment-lined large sheet pan.

2. In a medium mixing bowl, using an immersion blender or a whisk, whisk together the sugar, yogurt, and the oil, lemon zest, lemon juice, egg whites, vanilla, and salt until completely combined and the mixture looks silky and smooth.

3. Using a fine-mesh sieve, sift the flour and baking powder into a large bowl. Pour in the sugar mixture and whisk well until combined and smooth. Stir in the poppy seeds.

4. Pour the batter into the prepared muffin cups, filling them a little more than halfway.

5. Bake for 35–40 minutes or until the cakes have fully risen, the tops are golden brown, and a skewer inserted in the center of a cake comes out clean.

6. **MAKE THE SYRUP:** Note that the syrup must be hot when the cakes are done baking, so time this step accordingly. In a pot over medium-high heat, combine the sugar, corn syrup, water, lemon zest, and lemon juice. Bring to a boil, stirring, then lower the heat to low and simmer, stirring often, until the mixture is reduced by half and looks thick and syrupy, 5–8 minutes. Be sure to stir regularly so it doesn't stick to the bottom of the pot.

continued →

To Garnish

⅔ cup (150 ml) full-fat
unsweetened plain Greek
yogurt

½ cup (125 ml) Lemon Curd
(page 251)

7. As soon as the cakes come out of the oven, use a wooden skewer to poke a few holes in each cake, about three-quarters of the way down. Pour 1 tablespoon of hot syrup slowly and carefully onto each cake. Let cool to room temperature before removing the cakes from the molds.

8. Dollop some yogurt on top of each cake and swirl in some of the lemon curd. Devour promptly.

These cakes remain freshest when left in the molds, covered with plastic wrap, in the fridge for up to 7 days. After adding the syrup but before adding the toppings, they can also be individually wrapped and frozen for up to 3 months. They are best eaten at room temperature, so be sure to remove them from the fridge 40 minutes before you plan to serve them.

KITCHEN NOTE:

1. Silicone muffin trays are best for this recipe, as things get a little sticky with the syrup. If all you have is metal tins, line the cups with paper liners.

Vanilla Bean Cheesecake

Base

2 cups (250 g) graham cracker crumbs

3 Tbsp (45 ml) hot water (approx.)

3 Tbsp (45 g) unsalted butter, melted

Filling

1½ cups (375 g) Philadelphia-style cream cheese, at room temperature

1½ cups (300 g) granulated sugar

4 eggs, at room temperature

2 tsp pure vanilla extract

2 tsp vanilla bean paste (optional, see note)

¼ tsp kosher salt

½ cup (125 ml) full-fat sour cream, at room temperature

½ cup (125 ml) whipping cream, at room temperature (see note)

1 tsp finely grated lemon zest

There are many variations on cheesecake out there: those that are fluffy and light, those that are uncooked, and those that are denser and richer, like New York–style. Some are made with ricotta and some are made with cream cheese, but they are all finished and garnished with as much variety as there are people who bake them! Our cheesecake is somewhere in the middle of the various styles: creamy and fluffy, with a hint of tangy cheese, without being too dense or heavy. We make a different flavor each day at Crust, and I love that with this basic recipe, the topping options are endless. This one belongs in your repertoire, to garnish by season with chocolate, edible flowers, coulis, or fruit, making it a very impressive dessert!

1. Preheat the oven to 325°F (160°C). Spray or brush the bottom and sides of a 9-inch (23 cm) springform pan with a neutral oil, then line the bottom with parchment paper. Prepare a foil barrier (see note) and place the pan on top, in the middle of the foil sheets. Fold the foil up and press it against the sides of the pan.

2. **MAKE THE BASE:** In a medium mixing bowl, combine the graham crumbs, half of the hot water, and the butter. Mix until combined. Add more hot water as needed until the mixture just comes together to form a clump that holds its shape when you squeeze it in your palm.

3. Transfer the crumb mixture to the prepared pan and, using the back of a spoon, flatten it over the base so it's smooth and even. Bake for 15 minutes.

4. Meanwhile, put a full kettle of water on to boil (you will need 4–6 cups/1–1.5 L boiling water).

5. **MAKE THE FILLING:** Meanwhile, in a stand mixer, combine the cream cheese and sugar. Using the paddle attachment, beat on medium-low speed until well blended, 20–30 seconds. Increase the speed to medium-high and beat until smooth and creamy, 1–2 minutes. Stop the mixer and scrape down the sides of the bowl with a spatula. Make sure any chunks of cream cheese are scraped off the paddle. Mix on high speed for another 20–30 seconds to incorporate the unmixed bits.

6. Add the eggs, one at a time, continuously beating on low speed. Add the vanilla extract, vanilla bean paste (if using), and salt. Beat on low speed for 20 seconds to combine. Scrape down the bowl and beat on medium-high speed for another 10–15 seconds to ensure the mixture is very well combined. This will prevent unsightly lumps of cream cheese in the cake.

continued →

7. Add the sour cream, whipping cream, and lemon zest and mix on low speed until fully combined, 20–30 seconds. (Do not mix on a high speed or mix for too long, as that would aerate the mixture and you would end up with a cheese soufflé! That might sound good, but the cake would collapse after cooking and would look miserable when it cools.)

8. When the base is done baking, pour the cream cheese mixture over the base.

9. Place the springform pan, with the foil intact, in a large baking pan. Pour in enough boiling water to reach about 1 inch (2.5 cm) up the sides of the springform pan.

10. Bake for 45 minutes, then turn the baking pan 180 degrees to help the cake bake evenly. Bake for another 45–60 minutes, or until the top starts to rise evenly and becomes a very light golden brown. If the cake starts to color more than that before it starts to rise, cover it loosely with foil.

11. Carefully remove the baking pan from the oven and let cool to room temperature, about 45 minutes, before removing the cake from the water bath. Let the cake cool completely in the pan on a wire rack at room temperature for another hour, then place it in the fridge to set for 8 hours. (Cooling the cake slowly helps to prevent it from cracking.)

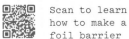 Scan to learn how to make a foil barrier

12. To serve, carefully remove the sides of the pan and use a slightly wet knife to cut the cake into slices, cleaning the knife between slices.

This cheesecake will keep, wrapped well with plastic wrap, for about 1 week in the fridge. I don't recommend freezing it, as it would lose some of its creamy texture.

KITCHEN NOTES:

1. If you don't have vanilla bean paste, feel free to leave it out—no need to replace it with more extract. Because vanilla is the star in this recipe, it's just nice to have the seeds from the paste flecked throughout the cake.

2. As with all cheesecakes, this comes together best if all the ingredients are at room temperature before mixing.

3. To create a foil barrier (scan the QR code for a how-to video) to make the springform pan somewhat waterproof and keep water out of your cheesecake, take two sheets of foil, each about 14 inches (35 cm) long, and lay one neatly on top of the other. Along one of the long sides, fold the two pieces to make a ½-inch (1.2 cm) crease, then repeat on the same crease twice more, for a total of three folds. Open the two sheets like a book and flatten well. You now have a 14-inch (35 cm) square piece of foil, with a seam down the middle, that is fairly watertight. Repeat with another two sheets of foil so you have two large squares. Place one square of foil on top of the other.

White Chocolate Strawberry Cheesecake

Strawberry Compote

1 cup (160 g) strawberries, sliced (see note)

¼ cup (50 g) granulated sugar

½ tsp finely grated lemon zest

4 Tbsp (60 ml) water, divided

1½ Tbsp (15 g) cornstarch

White Chocolate Honey Ganache

1 cup (180 g) white chocolate chips

¼ cup (70 ml) whipping cream (see note on page 108)

1 Tbsp good-quality honey

Base

2 cups (250 g) graham cracker crumbs

3 Tbsp (45 ml) hot water (approx.)

3 Tbsp (45 g) unsalted butter, melted

2 tsp rosewater (optional)

Filling

1½ cups (375 g) Philadelphia-style cream cheese, at room temperature

1 cup (200 g) granulated sugar

4 eggs, at room temperature

2 tsp pure vanilla extract

My kids and I often make this cake for Mother's Day, as the flavor combo is one of my wife, Pennye's, favorites, and it is very beautiful. It's a great way to use up overripe strawberries or the stash in the freezer you keep for occasions such as this. It's summery but can also be made when it's cold and damp out and you are craving a hit of strawberries. In other words, make this cake for any celebration throughout the year, and adorn it as you wish—with fresh berries and a ribbon of honey, or even edible flowers and more white chocolate if you like.

1. **MAKE THE COMPOTE:** In a medium saucepan, combine the strawberries, granulated sugar, lemon zest, and 2 tablespoons (30 ml) of the water. Cover with a tight-fitting lid and bring to a gentle simmer over medium heat, stirring occasionally (this will take 3–5 minutes).

2. In a small bowl, mix the cornstarch with the remaining 2 tablespoons (30 ml) water. Pour into the bubbling strawberry mixture, and simmer, stirring constantly, until the mixture has thickened, 60–90 seconds. Remove from heat and set aside.

3. **MAKE THE GANACHE:** Bring a medium pot with about 1 inch (2.5 cm) of water to a boil, then lower the heat to a simmer. Top with a stainless steel bowl that is just big enough to fit snugly on top of the pot without touching the water. Add the chocolate chips, whipping cream, and honey and stir gently with a spatula until silky smooth. (Alternatively, you can microwave the ingredients in a bowl for 20 seconds at a time, stirring well after each interval, for about 1 minute, until melted and smooth. With either method, be careful not to overheat it, or the chocolate will seize and won't be usable.)

4. Preheat the oven to 325°F (160°C). Spray or brush the bottom and sides of a 9-inch (23 cm) springform pan with a neutral oil, then line the bottom with parchment paper. Prepare a foil barrier (see note on page 108) and place the pan on top, in the middle of the foil sheets. Fold the foil up and press it against the sides of the pan.

5. **MAKE THE BASE:** In a medium mixing bowl, combine the graham crumbs, half of the hot water, and the butter and rosewater (if using). Mix until combined. Add more hot water as needed until the mixture just comes together to form a clump that holds its shape when you squeeze it in your palm.

6. Transfer the crumb mixture to the prepared pan and, using the back of a spoon, flatten it over the base so it's smooth and even. Bake for 15 minutes.

continued →

½ tsp finely grated
lemon zest

2 tsp fresh lemon juice

¼ tsp kosher salt

1¼ cups (300 ml) whipping
cream, at room temperature

<u>To Garnish</u>

1 cup (250 ml) sweetened
whipped cream

1 cup (160 g) strawberries,
halved, with stems
remaining

1 Tbsp good-quality honey,
for drizzling

2 tsp icing sugar, for
dusting

7. Meanwhile, put a full kettle of water on to boil (you will need 4–6 cups/1–1.5 L boiling water).

8. **MAKE THE FILLING:** Meanwhile, in a stand mixer, combine the cream cheese and granulated sugar. Using the paddle attachment, beat on medium-low speed until well blended, 20–30 seconds. Increase the speed to medium-high and beat until smooth and creamy, 1–2 minutes. Stop the mixer and scrape down the sides of the bowl with a spatula. Make sure any chunks of cream cheese are scraped off the paddle. Mix on high speed for another 20–30 seconds to incorporate the unmixed bits.

9. Add the eggs, one at a time, continuously beating on low speed. Add the vanilla, lemon zest, lemon juice, and salt. Beat on low speed for 20 seconds to combine. Scrape down the bowl and beat on medium-high speed for another 10 or 15 seconds to ensure the mixture is very well combined. This will prevent unsightly lumps of cream cheese in the cake.

10. Add the whipping cream and mix on low speed until fully combined, 20–30 seconds. (Do not mix on a high speed or mix for too long, as that would aerate the mixture and you would end up with a cheese soufflé! That might sound good, but the cake would collapse after cooking and would look miserable when it cools.)

11. When the base is done baking, pour the cream cheese mixture over the base. Spoon the strawberry compote on top and drizzle the ganache over the compote. Using a butter knife, swirl the three mixtures together a little.

12. Place the springform pan, with the foil intact, in a large baking pan. Pour in enough boiling water to reach about 1 inch (2.5 cm) up the sides of the springform pan.

13. Bake for 45 minutes, then turn the baking pan 180 degrees to help the cake bake evenly. Bake for another 45–60 minutes, or until the top starts to rise evenly and becomes a very light golden brown. If the cake starts to color more than that before it starts to rise, cover it loosely with foil.

14. Carefully remove the baking pan from the oven and let cool to room temperature, about 45 minutes, before removing the cake from the water bath. Let the cake cool completely in the pan on a wire rack at room temperature for another hour, then place it in the fridge to set for 8 hours. (Cooling the cake slowly helps to prevent it from cracking.)

15. To serve, carefully remove the sides of the pan. Pile the whipped cream and strawberries on top of the cake. Finish with a drizzle of honey and a sprinkle of icing sugar. Use a slightly wet knife to cut the cake into slices, cleaning the knife between slices.

    This cake will keep, wrapped well with plastic wrap, for up to 1 week in the fridge. To freeze it, firm it up in the freezer, unwrapped, for a few hours, then wrap it well with plastic wrap or foil, or place it in a large freezer bag, and store in the freezer for up to 1 month. The day before you plan to serve it, thaw it in the fridge.

KITCHEN NOTES:

1. If possible, use organic strawberries at the peak of their season (mid- to late summer). This will make a world of difference.

2. As with all cheesecakes, this comes together best if all the ingredients are at room temperature before mixing.

Mocha Cheesecake

Mocha

½ cup (90 g) semisweet dark chocolate chips

1 Tbsp cocoa powder

¼ cup (60 ml) strong hot black coffee (see note)

3 Tbsp (45 ml) coffee liqueur, such as Kahlúa or Tia Maria

Base

2 cups (250 g) graham cracker crumbs

2 Tbsp (16 g) cocoa powder, sifted

1 Tbsp granulated sugar

3 Tbsp (45 ml) hot water (approx.)

3 Tbsp (45 g) unsalted butter, melted

Filling

1½ cups (375 g) Philadelphia-style cream cheese, at room temperature

1½ cups (300 g) granulated sugar

4 eggs, at room temperature

1 tsp pure vanilla extract

¼ tsp kosher salt

1¼ cups (300 ml) whipping cream, at room temperature (see note)

My first wife, Crystal, and I originally opened our Canberra restaurant Sage as a café. However, as our customers became regulars and came to love our lunch menu, they began telling us what they really wanted from us: a fine-dining experience. We soon morphed to fit their needs, and suffice it to say we were all a little overwhelmed with Sage's popularity. There was often a mad scramble to find staff. At twenty-six years old, what could I do but recruit my mum to help? Twice a week, she would come in and we would bake a long list of cakes together. We baked for hours, coming up with different styles and flavors and combinations. We changed the cheesecake flavors regularly, and mocha emerged as one of the most popular. I will always remember this as a very special recipe from a very special time, with my mum by my side as I embarked on a huge adventure.

1. Preheat the oven to 325°F (160°C). Spray or brush the bottom and sides of a 9-inch (23 cm) springform pan with a neutral oil, then line the bottom with parchment paper. Prepare a foil barrier (see note on page 108) and place the pan on top, in the middle of the foil sheets. Fold the foil up and press it against the sides of the pan.

2. **MAKE THE MOCHA:** Pour the chocolate chips into a measuring jug. Using a fine-mesh sieve, sift the cocoa powder into the cup, then pour in the hot coffee. Let the ingredients sit and "get to know each other" for a minute or two, then mix them with a small whisk until smooth, about 30 seconds. Add the coffee liqueur and whisk until smooth. Let cool.

3. **MAKE THE BASE:** In a medium mixing bowl, combine the graham crumbs, cocoa, sugar, half of the hot water, and the butter. Mix until combined. Add more hot water as needed until the mixture just comes together to form a clump that holds its shape when you squeeze it in your palm.

4. Transfer the crumb mixture to the prepared pan and, using the back of a spoon, flatten it over the base so it's smooth and even. Bake for 15 minutes.

5. Meanwhile, put a full kettle of water on to boil (you will need 4–6 cups/1–1.5 L boiling water).

6. **MAKE THE FILLING:** Meanwhile, in a stand mixer, combine the cream cheese and sugar. Using the paddle attachment, beat on medium-low speed until well blended, 20–30 seconds. Increase the speed to medium-high and beat until smooth and creamy, 1–2 minutes. Stop the mixer and scrape down the sides of the bowl with a spatula. Make sure any chunks of cream cheese are scraped off the paddle. Mix on high speed for another 20–30 seconds to incorporate the unmixed bits.

continued →

7. Add the eggs, one at a time, continuously beating on low speed. Add the vanilla and salt. Beat on low speed for 20 seconds to combine. Scrape down the bowl and beat on medium-high speed for another 10 or 15 seconds to ensure the mixture is very well combined. This will prevent unsightly lumps of cream cheese in the cake.

8. Add the whipping cream and mix on low speed until fully combined, 20–30 seconds. (Do not mix on a high speed or mix for too long, as that would aerate the mixture and you would end up with a cheese soufflé! That might sound good, but the cake would collapse after cooking and would look miserable when it cools.)

9. Transfer about half of the cream cheese mixture to a separate mixing bowl. Add the mocha mixture and stir gently to combine—you don't want to incorporate too much air into the mixture by whisking it.

10. When the base is done baking, pour the remaining vanilla cream cheese mixture over the base. Pour the mocha cream cheese mixture in a spiral on top. Using a butter knife, swirl the two mixtures together, moving the knife back and forth and side to side three or four times, creating a pretty pattern without overmixing it.

11. Place the springform pan, with the foil intact, in a large baking pan. Pour in enough boiling water to reach about 1 inch (2.5 cm) up the sides of the springform pan.

12. Bake for 45 minutes, then turn the baking pan 180 degrees to help the cake bake evenly. Bake for another 45–60 minutes, or until the top starts to rise evenly and becomes a very light golden brown. If the cake starts to color more than that before it starts to rise, cover it loosely with foil.

13. Carefully remove the baking pan from the oven and let cool to room temperature, about 45 minutes, before removing the cake from the water bath. Let the cake cool completely in the pan on a wire rack at room temperature for another hour, then place it in the fridge to set for 8 hours. (Cooling the cake slowly helps to prevent it from cracking.)

14. To serve, carefully remove the sides of the pan and use a slightly wet knife to cut the cake into slices, cleaning the knife between slices.

This cake will keep, wrapped well with plastic wrap, for up to 1 week in the fridge. To freeze it, firm it up in the freezer, unwrapped, for a few hours, then wrap it well with plastic wrap or foil, or place it in a large freezer bag, and store in the freezer for up to 1 month. The day before you plan to serve it, thaw it in the fridge.

KITCHEN NOTES:

1. Instead of using strong brewed coffee, you can use 1 tablespoon of instant coffee granules mixed with ¼ cup (60 ml) boiling water.

2. As with all cheesecakes, this comes together best if all the ingredients are at room temperature before mixing.

Peach and Amaretto Cheesecake

Roasted Peaches

2 ripe medium-large freestone peaches, halved

¼ cup (50 g) light brown sugar, lightly packed

¼ cup (60 ml) amaretto liqueur, divided

1 tsp lime zest, finely grated

1 Tbsp fresh lime juice

Base

2 cups (250 g) graham cracker crumbs

¼ cup (25 g) whole almonds, toasted and finely crushed

3 Tbsp (45 ml) hot water (approx.)

3 Tbsp (45 g) unsalted butter, melted

Filling

1½ cups (375 g) Philadelphia-style cream cheese, at room temperature

1½ cups (300 g) granulated sugar

4 eggs, at room temperature

1 tsp pure vanilla extract

¼ tsp kosher salt

1¼ cups (300 ml) whipping cream, at room temperature (see note)

My wife, Pennye, and I love a little amaretto with a squeeze of lime at the end of a long week. Because my mind is constantly in creative mode, developing new flavors to bring to Crust and to my home kitchen, I find myself regularly inspired by what is around me, sometimes to the point of distraction. One summer evening, as we stood in our kitchen catching up over an amaretto, I found my attention wandering to the peaches on my counter. They were juicy and ultra-ripe, and the scent filled the warm kitchen, mingling with the amaretto and lime as I sipped. Boom! Sometimes these things come easily and are right in your face, ready for you to play and create!

1. Preheat the oven to 400°F (200°C).

2. **MAKE THE PEACHES:** Place the peach halves cut side up in a small, ovenproof glass or ceramic dish. Add the brown sugar, half of the amaretto, and the lime zest and juice and toss to coat. Cover the dish with foil.

3. Roast for about 60 minutes or until the peaches collapse and the juices begin to caramelize. Add the remaining amaretto, stir the peaches around in the caramelized juices, then let cool to room temperature. Cut the cooled peaches into ½-inch (1.2 cm) cubes, reserving the sauce from the dish. No need to peel the peaches, but if the skins are falling off, you can discard them.

4. Lower the oven temperature to 325°F (160°C). Spray or brush the bottom and sides of a 9-inch (23 cm) springform pan with a neutral oil, then line the bottom with parchment paper. Prepare a foil barrier (see note on page 108) and place the pan on top, in the middle of the foil sheets. Fold the foil up and press it against the sides of the pan.

5. **MAKE THE BASE:** In a medium mixing bowl, combine the graham crumbs, crushed almonds, half of the hot water, and the butter. Mix until combined. Add more hot water as needed until the mixture just comes together to form a clump that holds its shape when you squeeze it in your palm.

6. Transfer the crumb mixture to the prepared pan and, using the back of a spoon, flatten it over the base so it's smooth and even. Bake for 15 minutes.

7. Meanwhile, boil a full kettle of water (you will need 4–6 cups/1–1.5 L boiling water).

8. **MAKE THE FILLING:** Meanwhile, in a stand mixer, combine the cream cheese and granulated sugar. Using the paddle attachment, beat on medium-low speed until well blended, 20–30 seconds. Increase the speed to medium-high and beat until smooth and creamy, 1–2 minutes. Stop the mixer and scrape down the sides of the bowl with a spatula. Make sure any chunks of cream cheese are scraped off the paddle. Mix on high speed for another 20–30 seconds to incorporate the unmixed bits.

continued →

9. Add the eggs, one at a time, continuously beating on low speed. Add the vanilla and salt. Beat on low speed for 20 seconds to combine. Scrape down the bowl and beat on medium-high speed for another 10 or 15 seconds to ensure the mixture is very well combined. This will prevent unsightly lumps of cream cheese in the cake.

10. Add the whipping cream and mix on low speed until fully combined, 20–30 seconds. (Do not mix on a high speed or mix for too long, as that would aerate the mixture and you would end up with a cheese soufflé! That might sound good, but the cake would collapse after cooking and would look miserable when it cools.)

11. When the base is done baking, pour the cream cheese mixture over the base and arrange the peach pieces on top. Drizzle a few tablespoons of the peach amaretto sauce over top. Keep the remaining sauce for serving. You will notice that some of the peach pieces sink to the bottom as the cake bakes, and that's okay.

12. Place the springform pan, with the foil intact, in a large baking pan. Pour in enough boiling water to reach about 1 inch (2.5 cm) up the sides of the springform pan.

13. Bake for 45 minutes, then turn the baking pan 180 degrees to help the cake bake evenly. Bake for another 45–60 minutes, or until the top starts to rise evenly and becomes a very light golden brown. If the cake starts to color more than that before it starts to rise, cover it loosely with foil.

14. Carefully remove the baking pan from the oven and let cool to room temperature, about 45 minutes, before removing the cake from the water bath. Let the cake cool completely in the pan on a wire rack at room temperature for another hour, then place it in the fridge to set for 8 hours. (Cooling the cake slowly helps to prevent it from cracking.)

15. To serve, carefully remove the sides of the pan and use a slightly wet knife to cut the cake into slices, cleaning the knife between slices. Serve drizzled with the remaining peach amaretto sauce.

This cake will keep, wrapped well with plastic wrap, for up to 1 week in the fridge. To freeze it, firm it up in the freezer, unwrapped, for a few hours, then wrap it well with plastic wrap or foil, or place it in a large freezer bag, and store in the freezer for up to 1 month. The day before you plan to serve it, thaw it in the fridge.

KITCHEN NOTE:

1. As with all cheesecakes, this comes together best if all the ingredients are at room temperature before mixing.

Flourless Orange Almond Syrup Cake

Cake

3 large oranges, such as navel

1 cup (200 g) granulated sugar

5 eggs

2½ cups (300 g) almond flour, lightly packed

2 tsp baking powder (see note)

Orange Syrup

⅓ cup (120 g) orange marmalade

¾ cup (175 ml) fresh orange juice

½ cup (100 g) granulated sugar

To Garnish

Whipped cream

Dark Chocolate Ganache (page 244)

Toasted sliced almonds

Occasionally, you need to make a gluten-free and dairy-free cake. This one may be beyond any orange cake you've ever tasted, made with pure essence of cooked and blended whole oranges. Often, a dessert gets its orange flavor from a liqueur or orange water or a wee bit of zest, making for a mild tang. This cake, though, I call a punch-you-in-the-face orange cake, as the lovely orange flavor is strong, pure, and authentic.

1. **MAKE THE CAKE:** Place the whole, unpeeled oranges in a large saucepan and cover with cold water. Bring to a boil over high heat. Cover with a tight-fitting lid, turn the heat down to a gentle simmer, and cook for 2–3 hours or until the oranges look and feel soft, and fall apart easily when poked with a spoon. Check them regularly and top up the water as needed so that they don't boil dry and burn.

2. Preheat the oven to 350°F (180°C). Spray or brush a 9-inch (23 cm) springform pan with a neutral oil, and line the bottom and sides with parchment paper. Place it on a parchment-lined large rimmed sheet pan.

3. Drain the oranges and, while they are still in the strainer, use tongs to break them in half to help drain the liquid out of them. They must be completely drained. Let cool to room temperature in the strainer. Remove and discard the flower stalk, the core, and any seeds, along with any liquids. You will be left with the fruit and peel.

4. Place the orange fruit and peel in a blender. Add the sugar and blend for 2–3 minutes or until the oranges are completely puréed and look like an orange smoothie. Add the eggs and blend for 1 minute or until completely incorporated.

5. Pour the orange purée into a large mixing bowl. Add the almond flour and baking powder and whisk in well. It's impossible to overmix this batter because it doesn't contain any gluten!

6. Pour the batter into the prepared pan and gently smooth the top with a spatula.

7. Bake for 60–80 minutes, rotating it after 30 minutes to help it bake evenly, until the top is a rich golden brown and a skewer inserted in the center comes out clean. Keep an eye on it and tent it loosely with foil if it starts to get too dark before it is baked through.

continued →

8. **MAKE THE SYRUP:** Note that the syrup must be hot when the cake is done baking, so time this step accordingly. In a small saucepan, whisk together the marmalade, orange juice, and sugar. Bring to a rapid boil over high heat, stirring occasionally. Boil for 2–3 minutes, until the sugar has dissolved. Lower the heat to low and simmer gently until the syrup is sticky and slightly thickened, about 3 minutes. Test the viscosity by drizzling a few drops on a cool countertop—it needs to be sticky like honey when cool. If it isn't, continue cooking for 2–3 minutes.

9. As soon as the cake comes out of the oven, use a small knife to poke several holes in the top. Immediately pour the hot syrup evenly over the cake, ensuring it gets into the holes and drizzles over the sides. Let cool to room temperature on the sheet pan, 1–2 hours, then refrigerate for at least 2 hours, until set, before removing the cake from the springform pan.

10. Serve with whipped cream, dark chocolate ganache, and some toasted sliced almonds.

This cake will keep in an airtight container in the fridge for up to 1 week or in the freezer for up to 1 month. Thaw the frozen cake in the fridge overnight.

KITCHEN NOTE:

1. Make sure to use a gluten-free baking powder if you will be serving the cake to people with a gluten intolerance.

Lychee, Rosewater, and Raspberry Layer Cake

SERVES 12–14

Sponge Cakes

1½ cups (225 g) all-purpose flour

1 cup (120 g) cake or pastry flour (see page 12)

2 tsp baking powder

½ tsp kosher salt

1½ cups (300 g) granulated sugar

¾ cup (175 g) unsalted butter, softened

1 tsp pure vanilla extract

3 eggs, at room temperature

1½ cups (375 ml) buttermilk (see note)

Filling

2 cups (500 ml) whipping cream

½ cup (65 g) icing sugar

1½ tsp rosewater

1 tsp pure vanilla extract

To Assemble

1½ cups (375 ml) fresh raspberries, halved

1 cup (250 ml) roughly chopped seeded, peeled fresh lychees (or well-drained canned lychees, roughly chopped)

1 recipe Swiss Meringue (page 241; see note on page 39)

When I was a little kid, one of the first cookbooks I was ever given was a Disney cookbook, complete with recipes "by" Mickey, Donald, and several of the Disney princesses. It was then that I discovered Swiss meringue (a recipe by Snow White!), and I vaguely remember licking the creamy meringue from the beaters when my mum and I would make it. It was years before I would rediscover Swiss meringue, and the memories of baking with my mum came flooding back. This is a Disney princess–type cake: creamy and fruity, with the tang of raspberries, juicy lychees, and floral rosewater. At Crust, we make it a lot for birthdays and weddings, but as is my rule in general, cake requires no special occasion, so go ahead and bake it any time!

1. **MAKE THE CAKES:** Preheat the oven to 350°F (180°C). Spray or brush two 9-inch (23 cm) round cake pans with a neutral oil and line the bottoms with parchment paper.

2. Using a fine-mesh sieve, sift the all-purpose flour, pastry flour, baking powder, and salt into a medium bowl.

3. In a stand mixer, combine the granulated sugar, butter, and vanilla. Using the paddle attachment, beat on high speed until pale and creamy, 3–5 minutes. Add the eggs, one at a time, making sure each egg is fully incorporated before adding the next. Continue mixing on high speed until the mixture is smooth, light, and fluffy, another 1–2 minutes.

4. Add about one-third of the flour mixture and mix on medium-low speed until almost completely combined. Add about half of the buttermilk and mix on low speed until just combined. Add another third of the flour mixture and mix until just combined, increasing the speed if needed. Add the remaining buttermilk, then the remaining flour mixture, mixing until just combined and scraping down the bowl so everything is incorporated. Avoid overmixing. (This method helps prevent lumps from forming in the batter.)

5. Pour the batter evenly into the prepared pans and gently smooth the tops with a spatula.

6. Bake for 25–30 minutes, rotating the pans after about 15 minutes for even baking, until the cakes are light golden brown and a skewer inserted in the center of a cake comes out clean. Let cool in the pans on a wire rack for 10–15 minutes, then carefully transfer the cakes to the rack to cool completely, at least 1 hour.

continued →

7. **MAKE THE FILLING:** In the stand mixer, combine the whipping cream, icing sugar, rosewater, and vanilla. Using the whisk attachment, whisk until the mixture is thick and holds a stiff peak, 3–5 minutes.

8. **ASSEMBLE THE CAKE:** Using a serrated bread knife, trim off the top of each cooled cake so that it is 1 inch (2.5 cm) high. Cut each cake in half crosswise, giving you four layers, each ½ inch (1.2 cm) high and flat on the top and bottom (see note on page 96).

9. Starting with a cake layer with an uncut bottom, place it cut side up on a serving plate or cake stand. (Save the other round with an uncut bottom for the final layer; it's easier to frost and gives an even look to your finished cake.) Using a small offset spatula, spread one-third of the filling evenly over top. Sprinkle one-third each of the raspberries and lychees evenly over the filling.

10. Press a second cake layer firmly on top of the first, making sure it is level and flat. Spread another third of the filling on top, then sprinkle with another third of the raspberries and lychees. Repeat with a third cake layer and the remaining filling, raspberries, and lychees. Place the final layer cut side down. Carefully wrap the cake with plastic wrap and chill in the fridge for at least 1 hour or overnight.

11. Pile the meringue on top of the cake and, using a large spatula, spread it evenly over the top and sides (see note). Using the tip of the spatula, finish the meringue with a pretty pattern. Keep in the fridge, uncovered, until ready to serve, up to 2 hours. Serve cold.

The undressed sponge cakes will keep, well wrapped, in the freezer for up to 1 month. Thaw in the fridge overnight before assembling. The assembled layer cake will keep in an airtight container in the fridge for 2–3 days. I don't recommend freezing it once assembled.

KITCHEN NOTES:

1. If you don't have buttermilk, simply stir 2 teaspoons fresh lemon juice into whole milk a few minutes before you are ready to use it.

2. Make sure to scrape off any excess filling from the sides of the cake before finishing with the Swiss meringue. This will help the meringue stick to the cake and prevent it from sliding off.

Blackberry Almond Snacking Cake

Cake

1 cup (150 g) all-purpose flour (see note)

2 tsp baking powder

1 cup (120 g) almond flour, lightly packed

1 cup (225 g) unsalted butter, at room temperature

1 cup (200 g) granulated sugar

½ tsp kosher salt

3 eggs, at room temperature

½ tsp finely grated lemon zest

2 tsp fresh lemon juice

1 tsp pure vanilla extract

1½ cups (180 g) fresh or thawed frozen blackberries, divided (see note)

Blackberry Icing

1½ cups (195 g) icing sugar

3 Tbsp (45 ml) fresh blackberry juice, strained of any seeds

1 Tbsp unsalted butter, melted

1 tsp fresh lemon juice

Where I grew up, we had some lovely friends, the Olsons, who lived down the road. They had an orchard in their backyard, full of trees teeming with deep-red plums, plump orange apricots, and gorgeous Mission figs. Every year they would generously share their bounty with us, either in raw form or in a selection of wonderful baked goods. And man, could Mrs. Olson bake! One way she would use up her abundance of fruit was to make a simple white cake, toss a bunch of fruit on top, and let it bake into a big, delicious pudding. That's what this cake is all about. Simply made, quickly tossed together, and ready for snacking any time of day.

1. Preheat the oven to 350°F (180°C). Spray or brush a 10-inch (25 cm) square baking pan with a neutral oil and line it with parchment paper.

2. **MAKE THE CAKE:** Using a fine-mesh sieve, sift the flour and baking powder into a medium bowl. Stir in the almond flour.

3. In a stand mixer, combine the butter, granulated sugar, and salt. Using the paddle attachment, beat on low speed for 30 seconds, then increase to high speed and beat until well mixed and pale, about 2 minutes.

4. With the machine running on low speed, add the eggs, one at a time, fully incorporating each egg before adding the next. Scrape down the bowl so everything is incorporated. Add the lemon zest, lemon juice, and vanilla and mix on low speed until fully combined, about 30 seconds.

5. Remove the bowl from the stand and fold in the flour mixture until just combined.

6. Pour the batter into the prepared pan and gently smooth the top with a spatula. Evenly distribute 1 cup (125 g) of the blackberries on top.

7. Bake for 40 minutes, rotating it after 30 minutes to help it bake evenly, then cover loosely with foil and bake for another 10–15 minutes or until the cake has begun to rise a bit in the center and doesn't wobble, and a skewer inserted in the center comes out clean (see note). Be sure not to stick a skewer into a blackberry! Let cool completely in the pan on a wire rack.

continued →

8. **MAKE THE ICING:** In a small bowl, whisk together the icing sugar, blackberry juice, butter, and lemon juice until dissolved into a smooth icing.

9. Smear the icing over the cake and cut into sixteen slices. Serve cold or at room temperature with the remaining blackberries.

   This cake will keep in an airtight container at room temperature for 2–3 days or in the fridge for up to 1 week. You can also freeze it for up to 1 month before icing it. Thaw the frozen cake in the fridge overnight before icing and serving.

KITCHEN NOTES:

1. I love this cake because it is simple and flexible—it even works great if you replace the all-purpose flour with an equal amount of gluten-free flour.

2. You can use other fruits or berries, such as raspberries, halved summer apricots, pitted cherries, or halved blood-red plums, in place of the blackberries.

3. Be careful not to overbake this cake. It's at its best when it comes out moist with a little chew and a perfect crumb. It might look a little underdone at the top center, but if the skewer comes out clean, consider it ready!

Summer Fruit Pavlova

with Raspberry Curd

1 cup (200 g) granulated sugar

½ cup (125 ml) egg whites (about 4)

⅛ tsp kosher salt

2 tsp pure vanilla extract, divided

1½ cups (375 ml) whipping cream

1½ Tbsp (12 g) sifted icing sugar, plus 2 tsp for dusting

1 recipe Raspberry Curd (page 251)

1 cup (250 ml) cubed mango, cubed watermelon, or cherries

1 cup (250 ml) strawberries, halved

1 cup (250 ml) raspberries

½ cup (125 ml) blueberries

¼ cup (60 ml) small mint leaves

¼ cup (60 ml) fresh raspberry juice (optional)

We had a handful of chickens on the farm where I grew up (and one very scary rooster who would chase us around the yard!), so we always had the luxury of fresh eggs. With four of us kids, it wasn't a great chore to go through our daily eggs, but once in a while, we would find ourselves with several extras. The logical solution to the "problem"? Pavlova. Pavlova is taken very seriously in Australia, and I have a multitude of fond memories surrounding this famous dessert—mostly of my mum and my grandmother, shoulder to shoulder at the counter, preparing wonderful food for us all. Both of these special women have been a huge support and inspiration to me over the years. I dedicate this beautiful summer dessert to them.

1. Preheat the oven to 200°F (100°C). Line a large sheet pan with parchment paper. With a dark pen, trace an 8-inch (20 cm) circle on the parchment (a cake pan will do for your stencil), then flip the paper over so that the marker is on the underside.

2. In a medium heatproof bowl, whisk together the granulated sugar and egg whites.

3. Bring a medium pot with about 1 inch (2.5 cm) of water to a boil, then lower the heat to a simmer. Set the bowl of egg whites on top, ensuring the bottom doesn't touch the water. Warm the egg whites, stirring slowly and continuously, for about 5 minutes. The sugar will begin to dissolve and the mixture will clear. Keep stirring or you may end up with sweet scrambled egg whites! The liquid will feel quite warm, almost hot to the touch, 140–160°F (60–70°C), and the mixture will no longer be gritty when you rub a little between your fingertips. Carefully remove the bowl from the water bath and place it on a cloth to dry the bottom thoroughly so it doesn't drip water into the mix when you transfer it in the next step.

4. Pour the egg whites into a very clean stand mixer bowl. Add the salt and 1 teaspoon of the vanilla. Using the whisk attachment, whisk on high for about 5 minutes or until the sides of the bowl feel like they have cooled to room temperature and the mixture is light and fluffy and holds a stiff peak.

5. Pour the meringue into a neat pile in the center of the circle on the sheet pan. Using a small spatula, round off the meringue to fill the 8-inch (20 cm) circle. Make a shallow well in the center, leaving a thick layer on the bottom and sides to support all the curd, whipping cream, and fruit that will go inside once it's baked. You can get creative with the sides of the pavlova: neat sides, spiked sides—whatever you like.

continued →

6. Bake for 2 hours, then turn off the oven, leaving the pavlova inside with the door slightly open, for 1 hour. Remove from the oven and let cool completely. Store in an airtight container until you are ready to serve, for up to 1 week at room temperature.

7. In the stand mixer, combine the whipping cream, icing sugar, and the remaining vanilla. Beat on high for about 3 minutes or until the cream holds a stiff peak.

8. Place the pavlova carefully on a large serving platter. Spoon the raspberry curd into the well and gently spread it evenly (see note). Pile the whipped cream on top, then arrange the fruit on top of the cream, starting with the largest fruit and finishing with the smallest on top. Tuck the mint leaves among the fruit. Drizzle with raspberry juice (if using) and dust with icing sugar. Serve immediately.

Once assembled, this pavlova is best eaten right away, but it can be kept in an airtight container in the fridge for 2–3 days. It may lose its structure a bit, but will still taste good!

KITCHEN NOTES:

1. Feel free to change the fruits for whatever you have on hand.

2. When adding the curd in step 8, remember that you will be placing fruit on top and don't want the curd to overflow. You may have extra curd, depending on how deep the well of your pavlova is.

KITCHEN NOTES:

1. Make sure the cakes are completely cool and the frosting is cold from the fridge before assembling. This is really important! Otherwise, the frosting will melt into a drippy disaster.

2. You can find special knives and measuring tools that help to slice a cake crosswise with razor-sharp accuracy. You can also measure and mark the cake with toothpicks or wrap a bit of kitchen twine around the cake to mark the spot to start slicing. The last thing you want after baking such a beauty is to slice it all off-balance!

3. I like to ice the cake "naked-style"–keeping the frosting light on the sides and top, with a bit of the cake showing through.

Signature Carrot Cake

2½ cups (375 g) all-purpose flour

1 tsp baking powder

½ tsp baking soda

4 eggs, at room temperature

1 cup (250 ml) vegetable oil

1 tsp finely grated orange zest

⅓ cup (75 ml) fresh orange juice

1½ cups (300 g) light brown sugar, lightly packed

2 cups (260 g) grated peeled carrots

1 cup (100 g) fresh or thawed frozen cranberries

½ cup (90 g) white chocolate chips

½ cup (50 g) toasted flaked almonds

1 recipe Lemon Cream Cheese Frosting (page 243)

My parents would often host dinner parties, allowing us four kids to make the food! I loved doing this, and while it may seem a bit risky to leave the success of a dinner party to your kids, what better way to teach them to cook? My brother and I were always responsible for dessert. We'd make outlandish things like baklava, sorbets, and pavlova, which took time and technique, but judging from the oohs and aahs coming from the dining room, we pulled it off quite well. One of the desserts we'd make often was a version of this carrot cake, and it was popular with our parents' friends. I've changed it up a bit since then, adding fresh orange juice and zest, plus white chocolate for extra decadence.

1. Preheat the oven to 350°F (180°C). Spray or brush two 9-inch (23 cm) round cake pans with a neutral oil, then line them with parchment paper.

2. Using a fine-mesh sieve, sift the flour, baking powder, and baking soda into a bowl.

3. In a large measuring jug, using an immersion blender, mix the eggs, oil, and orange juice until well combined, about 10 seconds. (If you don't have an immersion blender, briskly whisk the ingredients together.) Add the sugar and mix for 10 seconds or until it is dissolved.

4. Pour the egg mixture into a large mixing bowl and add the flour mixture and the orange zest, carrots, cranberries, chocolate chips, and almonds. Using a spatula, gently fold all the ingredients together until just combined. Be careful not to overmix.

5. Divide the batter between the cake tins, and using a small spatula, even out the surface of the cake.

6. Bake for 35–40 minutes, rotating the pans after about 25 minutes for even baking, until a skewer inserted in the center of a cake comes out clean. Let cool in the pans on a wire rack for 1 hour, then carefully transfer the cakes to the rack to cool completely (see note).

7. Using a serrated bread knife, trim off the top of each cooled cake so that it is level. Cut each cake in half crosswise, giving you four layers (see note).

8. Starting with a cake layer with an uncut bottom, place it cut side up on a serving plate or cake stand. (Save the other round with an uncut bottom for the final layer; it's easier to frost and gives an even look to your finished cake.) Using a small offset spatula, spread a little less than one-quarter of the frosting evenly over top (after frosting each layer, you'll want to have enough to finish the top and sides).

9. Press a second cake layer firmly on top of the first, making sure it is level and flat. Spread the same amount of frosting over top, keeping it flat and even. Repeat with another layer. Place the final layer cut side down and finish the top and sides of the cake with the remaining frosting. Cover loosely with plastic wrap and chill in the fridge for at least 2 hours before serving.

This cake will keep in an airtight container at room temperature for up to 2 days, in the fridge for up to 1 week, or in the freezer for up to 1 month.

Strawberry Friands

1 cup (130 g) sifted
icing sugar, plus more
for dusting

1 cup (120 g) almond flour,
lightly packed (see note)

½ cup (75 g) all-purpose
flour

¾ cup (175 g) unsalted
butter, melted

¾ cup (175 ml) egg whites
(about 6), lightly whisked

1 tsp pure vanilla extract

3 Tbsp (60 g) strawberry
jam, divided

12 medium strawberries,
each sliced evenly
lengthwise into 3 slices

Friands originated in France but have become a very popular treat in Australia. I started making them because, with so much lemon curd, brûlée, and other yolk-heavy desserts in my life, I needed a way to use up all those egg whites! Friands are moist, buttery, rich, and dense, partly thanks to the addition of almond flour. They are like delicate little cakes, reminiscent of madeleines. This is a one-bowl recipe, making it easy to throw together when you find yourself with extra egg whites on hand.

1. In a large bowl, using a spatula, gently mix the sugar, almond flour, all-purpose flour, butter, egg whites, and vanilla until just combined. Cover and refrigerate for 30 minutes. (The batter will keep in the fridge for a few days if you want to make it ahead of time.)

2. Meanwhile, preheat the oven to 350°F (180°C). Spray a 12-cup nonstick friand pan with a neutral oil or rub the cups with a little softened butter (see note).

3. Spoon the batter into the prepared pan, dividing evenly. Using the back of a teaspoon, make a small well in the top of each and place ½ teaspoon of the strawberry jam in each well. Top each friand with three strawberry slices.

4. Bake for 25–30 minutes or until the friands are light golden brown on the top and sides, and a skewer inserted in the center of a friand comes out clean. Let cool in the pan on a wire rack for 5 minutes, then transfer the friands to the rack to cool completely.

5. Combine the remaining strawberry jam with 1 teaspoon of hot water. Brush the top of each friand with the mixture. Dust with a little icing sugar and serve at room temperature.

These friands are best eaten the day they are baked, but will keep in a covered container at room temperature for up to 2 days or in the fridge for up to 1 week, or can be individually wrapped and stored in the freezer for up to 2 months.

KITCHEN NOTES:

1. You can substitute different nut flours, such as pistachio or hazelnut, 1:1. You can also mix up the fruit. I like to make blueberry pistachio or chocolate hazelnut friands. This recipe is fabulous because it's quick, easy, and very flexible.

2. A friand pan is rather specific, I know. It's very similar to a muffin tin, but the holes are oval and straight-edged. If you don't have one, I understand! Instead, you can use a 12-cup muffin tin or a mini loaf pan. Even a madeleine pan will do, but you'll need to adjust the baking time, as madeleine pans are generally quite a bit shallower. My preference is to use a silicone friand mold, lightly sprayed with a neutral oil. Play around and find your favorite.

Gingerbread Guinness Cake

1½ cups (375 ml) Guinness, or your favorite dark stout

½ cup (125 ml) pure maple syrup

2 Tbsp (30 ml) fancy molasses

2 tsp baking soda

2 cups (300 g) all-purpose flour

2 Tbsp (12 g) ground ginger

1 Tbsp ground cinnamon

1 tsp baking powder

1 tsp ground nutmeg

½ tsp ground cloves

½ tsp ground cardamom

½ cup (100 g) dark brown sugar, lightly packed

½ cup (100 g) granulated sugar

3 eggs

1 cup (250 ml) vegetable oil

2 tsp pure vanilla extract

½ tsp finely grated lemon zest

⅓ cup (50 g) finely chopped candied ginger

1 recipe Lemon Cream Cheese Frosting (page 243)

There are those winter months where there is a pleasant lull in the busyness: things have slowed down a bit, it gets dark early, a fire becomes necessary, and maybe it's even snowing outside. This cake scents the house with rich, deep notes of malty, spicy goodness, moistened with Guinness beer. The heavy, dark stout gives it a mystery flavor that is hard to place (unless you know). May I suggest that it's not too much to enjoy a Guinness alongside a piece!

1. Preheat the oven to 350°F (180°C). Spray or brush an 8 × 12-inch (20 × 30 cm) cake pan with a neutral oil and line it with parchment paper.

2. In a large saucepan, combine the Guinness, maple syrup, and molasses. Bring to a boil over medium-high heat, stirring occasionally. Remove from the heat and whisk in the baking soda. Be careful, as the mixture will bubble up rapidly. Let cool to room temperature.

3. Using a fine-mesh sieve, sift the flour, ground ginger, cinnamon, baking powder, nutmeg, cloves, and cardamom into a large bowl. Stir in the brown sugar and granulated sugar.

4. Make a well in the middle of the flour mixture and pour in the Guinness mixture. Add the eggs, oil, vanilla, lemon zest, and candied ginger to the well and stir until well combined.

5. Pour the batter into the prepared pan and gently smooth the top with a small spatula.

6. Bake for 50–55 minutes, rotating the pan after 25 minutes to ensure even baking, until deep golden brown and a skewer inserted in the center comes out clean. You may need to tent the cake loosely with foil for the last 10–15 minutes or so if you find it is getting too dark around the edges. Let cool to room temperature in the pan on a wire rack.

7. Frost the top of the cake with the lemon cream cheese frosting. Cut into twenty pieces. This cake is fabulous eaten at room temperature or chilled.

This cake will keep in an airtight container at room temperature for 3–5 days, in the fridge for up to 2 weeks, or in the freezer for up to 2 months.

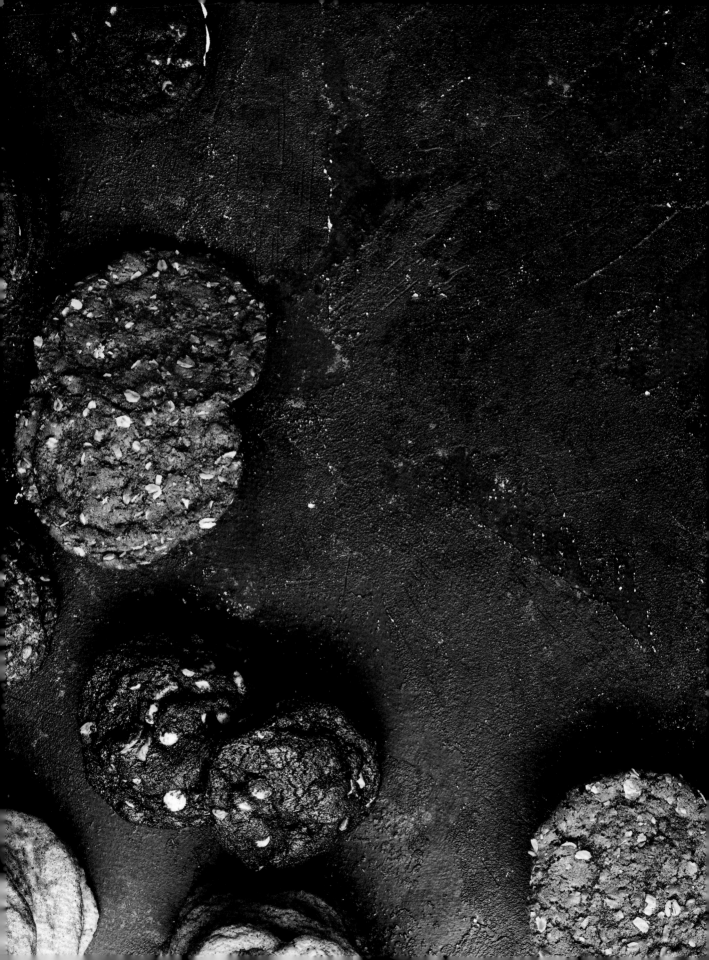

Cookies

"Funny, how one good cookie could calm the mind
and even elevate a troubled soul."

DEAN KOONTZ

KITCHEN NOTES:

1. When you mix in the cold eggs, the mixture will curdle a bit, and that's exactly what you want! This prevents too much air from getting into the batter, which makes pleasantly flat and chewy cookies rather than big puffy ones.

2. Before rolling in cinnamon sugar and baking, you can freeze the dough balls on the sheet pan, then transfer them to a freezer bag, squeezing out as much air as possible, and store in the freezer for up to 1 month. Thaw at room temperature for about 20 minutes, then keep cold in the fridge while each batch bakes.

Ginger Chew Cookies

Cookies

3¾ cups (560 g) all-purpose flour

3 tsp ground ginger

2½ tsp baking soda

2 tsp ground cinnamon

½ tsp ground cloves

3 cups (600 g) granulated sugar

¾ cup (175 g) unsalted butter, at room temperature

½ cup (125 ml) fancy molasses

½ tsp kosher salt

3 eggs, cold

1 tsp pure vanilla extract

⅓ cup (50 g) finely chopped candied ginger

Cinnamon Sugar

½ cup (100 g) granulated sugar

1 Tbsp ground cinnamon

Back in the day, ginger snaps were my favorite. I still love them with tea, as their hard, snappy texture requires a dip for sure. For Crust, I wanted to make something with the same flavor profile that didn't cause our customers to break their teeth! We decided to make a chewy version, with layers of ginger flavor from both ground ginger and candied pieces. These cookies are big and lovely and rich, so they are great for sharing. And if you are so inclined, they can certainly be dipped as well.

1. Line two large sheet pans with parchment paper.

2. **MAKE THE COOKIES:** Using a fine-mesh sieve, sift the flour, ground ginger, baking soda, cinnamon, and cloves into a small bowl.

3. In a stand mixer, combine the sugar, butter, molasses, and salt. Using the paddle attachment, beat on high speed until pale and creamy, about 2 minutes. Add the eggs and vanilla and mix on medium-low speed for about 30 seconds (don't worry if it curdles; see note). Add the flour mixture and mix on low speed until just combined, about 20 seconds.

4. Remove the bowl from the stand and stir in the candied ginger, scraping down the bowl so all is combined.

5. **MAKE THE CINNAMON SUGAR:** In a large shallow bowl, combine the sugar and cinnamon and mix well.

6. Using a soup spoon or a cookie scoop, form the dough into twenty-four equal-sized balls. Roll each ball in cinnamon sugar until well coated. Place them all on one of the prepared pans (they can be close together). Cover with plastic wrap and refrigerate for 30 minutes.

7. Meanwhile, preheat the oven to 350°F (180°C).

8. Transfer six balls to the second prepared pan, giving them room to spread. Gently press down on the cookies with your fingertips, just enough so they don't roll away. Keep the remaining dough balls in the fridge until ready to bake.

9. Bake for 12–14 minutes, rotating the pan after 6 minutes, until the cookies are slightly cracked on top. Take them out a bit earlier if you like them chewy, or a bit later if you like them crispier. Let cool on the pan for 5 minutes, then transfer the cookies to a wire rack to cool completely.

10. Repeat steps 8 and 9 three more times with the remaining dough balls.

These cookies will keep in an airtight container at room temperature for up to 3 days or in the freezer for up to 2 months.

Diablo Cookies

1⅔ cups (250 g) all-purpose flour

½ cup (50 g) cocoa powder

½ tsp baking soda

2 tsp chili powder

1½ tsp ground ginger

1 tsp kosher salt

1 tsp ground cinnamon

½ tsp cayenne pepper (optional, see note)

½ tsp ground cardamom

1 cup (225 g) unsalted butter, at room temperature

½ cup + 2 Tbsp (120 g) light brown sugar, lightly packed

¾ cup (150 g) granulated sugar

1 Tbsp fancy molasses

2 eggs, cold

½ tsp pure vanilla extract

½ tsp finely grated orange zest

¾ cup (135 g) semisweet chocolate chips

1 tsp flaky sea salt, such as Vancouver Island Sea Salt or Maldon salt

In 2010, I took a trip to Spain. As one does, I spent much of the trip eating, drinking, and taking in all the incredible pleasures that Spain has to offer. Although the paella and the gazpacho were undoubtedly memorable, what I couldn't stop thinking about when I returned home was the enchanting combination of chocolate, salt, and chili powder that I first experienced in the form of a cookie. (Several cookies, if I'm being honest!) I promised myself I would recreate these cookies once I returned home, and while nothing compares to the originals, I think these come pretty close to their Spanish counterparts.

1. Line two large sheet pans with parchment paper.

2. Using a fine-mesh sieve, sift the flour, cocoa, baking soda, chili powder, ginger, kosher salt, cinnamon, cayenne (if using), and cardamom into a medium bowl.

3. In a stand mixer, combine the butter, brown sugar, granulated sugar, and molasses. Using the paddle attachment, beat on medium speed until soft, pale, and creamy like mayonnaise, about 3 minutes. Turn the mixer off and add the eggs and vanilla. Mix on low speed until just combined, about 1 minute (don't worry if it curdles; see note on page 138).

4. Scrape down the bowl with a spatula, then add the flour mixture and the orange zest. Mix on low speed until just combined, about 30 seconds.

5. Remove the bowl from the stand and gently fold in the chocolate chips. Using a large spatula, scrape down the bowl so all is combined. Be careful not to overmix.

6. Using a soup spoon or a cookie scoop, form the dough into sixteen balls, about 2 ounces (60 g) each. Place them all on one of the prepared pans (they can be close together). Cover with plastic wrap and refrigerate for 1 hour.

7. Meanwhile, preheat the oven to 350°F (180°C).

8. Transfer six balls to the second prepared pan, giving them room to spread. Gently press down on each cookie to flatten slightly. Keep the remaining dough balls in the fridge until ready to bake.

9. Sprinkle each cookie with a pinch of flaky sea salt. I like to be able to taste and feel the salt as I eat these cookies, so I'm quite generous with it, but use as much or as little as you prefer. Work quickly, as you want the dough to remain cold.

10. Bake for 9–11 minutes, rotating the pan after 5 minutes. The cookies will get a wee bit crispier the longer you bake them. I like mine a little underdone and chewy! Let cool on the pan for 10–15 minutes, then transfer the cookies to a wire rack to cool completely.

11. Repeat steps 8–10 twice more with the remaining dough balls (you will only have four cookies in the third batch).

These cookies will keep in an airtight container at room temperature for up to 3 days or in the freezer for up to 2 months.

KITCHEN NOTE:

1. You can make these cookies as spicy as you like, or you can skip the cayenne completely. Do yourself a favor, though, and try at least one batch with the heat included. It is truly a wicked combination.

Abby's Chocolate
Crinkle Cookies

1 cup (150 g) all-purpose
flour

⅓ cup (35 g) cocoa powder

1 tsp baking powder

½ tsp kosher salt

¼ tsp baking soda

3 eggs

1½ cups (300 g) dark brown
sugar, lightly packed

1 tsp pure vanilla extract

¼ cup (60 g) unsalted
butter

⅔ cup (120 g) bittersweet
chocolate chips

½ cup (100 g) granulated
sugar

½ cup (65 g) icing sugar

My daughter, Abby, makes a lot of cookies. As her baker dad, I try to teach her my ways, but Abby likes to do things the way she likes to do things—as any parent will be familiar with! I watch her furrow her brow in determination as she declines my help. I see her try and fail, and I bite my tongue as I allow her this independence. I beam as she tries again, and again, until ultimate success is achieved! And I commiserate with her when it isn't, because that is baking, and life isn't perfect. I am so proud of Abby and love that I can sell her delicious cookies at the bakery and now share them here with you. We eat these cookies a ton; they go especially well with hot tea or coffee for a sweet afternoon break.

1. Preheat the oven to 325°F (160°C). Line two large sheet pans with parchment paper.

2. Using a fine-mesh sieve, sift the flour, cocoa, baking powder, salt, and baking soda into a medium bowl.

3. In a large bowl, whisk together the eggs, brown sugar, and vanilla.

4. Bring a medium pot with about 1 inch (2.5 cm) of water to a boil, then lower the heat to a simmer. Top with a stainless steel bowl that is just big enough to fit snugly on top of the pot without touching the water. Add the butter and chocolate chips and stir gently with a spatula until silky smooth. (Alternatively, you can microwave the chocolate and butter in a bowl for 20 seconds at a time, stirring well after each interval, for about 1 minute, until melted and smooth. With either method, be careful not to overheat it, or the chocolate will seize and won't be usable.)

5. Slowly add about ¼ cup of the chocolate mixture to the egg mixture, whisking constantly so the eggs don't cook on contact with the hot chocolate. Whisk in the remaining chocolate mixture until well combined. Using a rubber spatula, gently stir in the flour mixture until combined. Let sit at room temperature for 10 minutes.

6. Place the granulated sugar in one shallow bowl and the icing sugar in another.

7. Using a soup spoon or a 2-ounce cookie scoop, form the dough into eighteen equal-sized balls. Drop each ball in the granulated sugar and roll to coat, then roll in the icing sugar. (This might seem like a lot of sugar, but trust me, it makes the cookies crack beautifully!) Place six balls on each of the prepared pans, leaving about 3 inches (8 cm) between them to give them space to spread (two rows of three on each pan works well).

continued →

9. Bake for about 10 minutes, rotating the pan after 6 minutes, or until the cookies start to puff a little and the tops begin to crack. The baking time will depend on your oven and your taste! Experiment with anywhere between 9 and 12 minutes. If you like them chewier, don't be fooled if they look under-baked at 9–10 minutes—they will set perfectly once they're out of the oven. Let cool on the pan for 5–10 minutes, then transfer the cookies to a wire rack to cool completely.

10. Repeat steps 8 and 9 three more times with the remaining dough balls.

    These cookies will keep in an airtight container at room temperature for up to 3 days or in the freezer for up to 2 months.

KITCHEN NOTE:

1. If you want to prepare the dough ahead of time, complete through step 5, then cover the bowl tightly with plastic wrap and pop it in the fridge. It will happily wait for you there for up to 3 days. After forming the dough into balls as described in step 6, let them rest at room temperature for about 30 minutes before baking.

Oatmeal Raisin Cookies

1½ cups (225 g) all-purpose flour

2 tsp ground cinnamon

2 tsp baking soda

1 cup (225 g) unsalted butter, at room temperature

1 cup (200 g) light brown sugar, lightly packed

½ cup (100 g) granulated sugar

1 tsp kosher salt

2 eggs, cold

1 tsp pure vanilla extract

2 cups (180 g) old-fashioned rolled oats

1½ cups (225 g) raisins

The oatmeal raisin cookie is a staple. While it is not groundbreaking, I consider it to be like a cup of tea or a simple salad. If done right, with the perfect combination of ingredients and technique, it can be exceptional. This one packs a lot of flavor, is crispy on the outside and chewy on the inside, and, right out of the oven, is a wonderful accompaniment to an afternoon break. At Crust, we can barely keep them on the shelf! A super classic that most people cannot resist, even those who are not raisin lovers.

1. Line two large sheet pans with parchment paper.

2. Using a fine-mesh sieve, sift the flour, cinnamon, and baking soda into a small bowl.

3. In a stand mixer, combine the butter, brown sugar, granulated sugar, and salt. Using the paddle attachment, beat on high speed until pale and creamy, about 2 minutes. Add the eggs and vanilla and mix on medium-low speed for about 10 seconds (don't worry if it curdles; see note on page 138). Add the flour mixture and mix on low speed until just combined, about 20 seconds.

4. Remove the bowl from the stand and stir in the oats and raisins, scraping down the bowl so all is combined.

5. Using a soup spoon or a cookie scoop, form the dough into twenty balls, about 2 ounces (60 g) each. Place them on one of the prepared pans (they can be close together). Cover with plastic wrap and refrigerate for 30 minutes.

6. Meanwhile, preheat the oven to 350°F (180°C).

7. Transfer five balls to the second prepared pan, giving them room to spread. Gently press down on the cookies with your fingertips, just enough so they don't roll away. Keep the remaining dough balls in the fridge until ready to bake.

8. Bake for 11–13 minutes, rotating the pan after 6 minutes, until the cookies are deep golden brown. Take them out a bit earlier if you like them chewy, or a bit later if you like them crispier. Let cool on the pan for 5 minutes, then transfer the cookies to a wire rack to cool completely.

9. Repeat steps 7 and 8 three more times with the remaining dough balls.

These cookies will keep in an airtight container at room temperature for up to 3 days or in the freezer for up to 2 months.

KITCHEN NOTE:

1. Before baking, you can freeze the dough balls on the sheet pan, transfer them to a freezer bag, and freeze for up to 1 month. Thaw at room temperature for about 20 minutes, then bake.

KITCHEN NOTES:

1. Before baking, you can freeze the dough balls on the sheet pan, then transfer them to a freezer bag, squeezing out as much air as possible, and store in the freezer for up to 1 month. Thaw at room temperature for about 20 minutes, then bake.

2. These cookies can be halved in size to make double the amount. Use a 1-ounce cookie scoop so each cookie ball is about 1 ounce (30 g). Bake for about 9 minutes.

Double Chocolate Pistachio Cookies

1½ cups (225 g) all-purpose flour

½ cup (50 g) cocoa powder

½ tsp baking soda

1 cup (225 g) unsalted butter, at room temperature

½ cup + ⅓ cup (170 g) light brown sugar, lightly packed

⅔ cup (130 g) granulated sugar

1 Tbsp fancy molasses

1 tsp kosher salt

2 eggs, cold

1 tsp pure vanilla extract

¾ cup (135 g) white chocolate chips

1 cup (160 g) unsalted pistachios, roughly chopped

A local vendor who visits Crust regularly eats one of these cookies every day before his shift starts. We give him the scraps of cookies that break (which can sometimes be quite a few!), but if there are none, we happily slip him a whole cookie or two. He is a happy-go-lucky kind of guy, always smiling and cheerful, with a kind soul and a giving heart. I don't think it's a stretch to think that these cookies, which he has proven are great for breakfast, might be the reason for his sunny demeanor!

1. Line two large sheet pans with parchment paper.

2. Using a fine-mesh sieve, sift the flour, cocoa, and baking soda into a small bowl.

3. In a stand mixer, combine the butter, brown sugar, granulated sugar, molasses, and salt. Using the paddle attachment, beat on high speed until pale and creamy, about 2 minutes. Add the eggs and vanilla and mix on medium-low speed for about 30 seconds (don't worry if it curdles; see note on page 138). Add the flour mixture and mix on low speed until just combined, about 20 seconds.

4. Remove the bowl from the stand and stir in the chocolate chips and pistachios, scraping down the bowl so all is combined.

5. Using a soup spoon or a 2-ounce cookie scoop, form the dough into twenty equal-sized balls. Place them all on one of the prepared pans (they can be close together). Cover with plastic wrap and refrigerate for 30 minutes.

6. Meanwhile, preheat the oven to 350°F (180°C).

7. Transfer ten balls to the second prepared pan, giving them room to spread. Gently press down on the cookies with your fingertips, just enough so they don't roll away. Keep the remaining dough balls in the fridge until ready to bake.

8. Bake for 12–14 minutes, rotating the pan after 6 minutes, until the cookies are slightly cracked on top. Take them out a bit earlier if you like them chewy, or a bit later if you like them crispier. Let cool on the pan for 5 minutes, then transfer the cookies to a wire rack to cool completely.

9. Spread out the remaining dough balls on their pan and gently press down on each. Repeat step 8.

These cookies will keep in an airtight container at room temperature for up to 3 days or in the freezer for up to 2 months.

Snickerdoodles

2⅓ cups (350 g) all-purpose flour

1 tsp baking soda

2 cups (400 g) granulated sugar, divided

1 cup (225 g) unsalted butter, at room temperature

½ tsp kosher salt

2 eggs, cold

½ tsp pure vanilla extract

2 tsp ground cinnamon

Snickerdoodles were not something I'd heard of until one of my kids came home from a friend's house with a box of these delicious morsels. I love how simple they are, sort of like a chocolate chip cookie without the chocolate and with a hint of cinnamon. Despite their silly name, snickerdoodles are a very earnest cookie, and I've never met anyone who doesn't love them, so they've become a Crust staple since we opened our doors in 2013. My staff know them so well, they could practically make them with their eyes closed!

1. Line two large sheet pans with parchment paper.

2. Using a fine-mesh sieve, sift the flour and baking soda into a bowl.

3. In a stand mixer, combine 1½ cups (300 g) of the sugar and the butter and salt. Using the paddle attachment, mix on medium-high speed until well combined, pale, and creamy, about 2 minutes. Add the eggs and vanilla and mix on medium-low speed to combine, about 10 seconds (don't worry if it curdles; see note on page 138).

4. Turn the mixer off and add the flour mixture. Using a very low speed, mix until it is all combined, about 20 seconds. Using a spatula, scrape down the sides of the bowl to the bottom to make sure you've mixed in all pockets of butter. Gently fold in any you missed.

5. In a small mixing bowl, whisk together the remaining ½ cup (100 g) sugar and the cinnamon.

6. Using a soup spoon or a cookie scoop, form the dough into fourteen balls, about 2 ounces (60 g) each. Drop each ball in the cinnamon sugar and roll to coat evenly and generously. Place them all on one of the prepared pans (they can be close together). Let rest, uncovered, at room temperature for about 10 minutes.

7. Meanwhile, preheat the oven to 350°F (180°C).

8. Transfer seven balls to the second prepared pan, giving them room to double in size. Gently press down on the cookies with your fingertips, just enough so they don't roll away. Keep the remaining dough balls covered at room temperature until ready to bake.

9. Bake for 12–14 minutes, rotating the pan after 6 minutes, until the cookies are slightly cracked on top. Take them out a bit earlier if you like them chewy, or a bit later if you like them crispier. Let cool on the pan for about 10 minutes, then carefully transfer the cookies to a wire rack to cool completely.

10. Spread out the remaining dough balls on their pan and gently press down on each. Repeat step 9.

    These cookies will keep in an airtight container at room temperature for up to 3 days or in the freezer for up to 2 months.

KITCHEN NOTE:

1. Before rolling in cinnamon sugar and baking, you can freeze the dough balls on the sheet pan, then transfer them to a freezer bag, squeezing out as much air as possible, and store in the freezer for up to 1 month. Thaw at room temperature for about 20 minutes, roll in cinnamon sugar, then keep cold in the refrigerator while each batch bakes.

Speculoos

½ cup + 2 Tbsp (90 g)
all-purpose flour

⅔ cup (100 g) cake or
pastry flour (see page 12)

⅔ cup (100 g) whole wheat
flour

½ tsp baking soda

½ tsp ground cinnamon

1 cup (225 g) unsalted
butter, at room temperature

½ cup (100 g) dark brown
sugar, lightly packed

⅓ cup (70 g) granulated
sugar

1 tsp good-quality honey

½ tsp kosher salt

2 Tbsp (30 ml) raspberry jam

1 Tbsp icing sugar,
for dusting

Speculoo, despite rhyming with "kangaroo," is not an Australian cookie! In my cookie research days, before opening Crust, I came across this sort of whole wheat cinnamon-scented shortbread. It really appealed to me, and I knew it would be popular with our customers too. Speculoos come in all shapes and sizes, often cut decoratively or made by pressing the dough into a mold. I decided to put a spot of jam in the middle of my simply shaped speculoos to honor my maternal grandmother. She was famous for her jam drop cookies (grandmothers tend to have a claim to fame—often from the kitchen), and I think of her when I make these. It's funny how we tend to weave our love for our families into our cooking and baking, isn't it?

1. Using a fine-mesh sieve, sift the all-purpose flour, cake flour, whole wheat flour, baking soda, and cinnamon into a bowl.

2. In a stand mixer, combine the butter, brown sugar, granulated sugar, honey, and salt. Using the paddle attachment, mix on medium-high speed until well combined, pale, and creamy, about 2 minutes. With the mixer on low speed, add half of the flour mixture, wait about 15 seconds, then add the remaining flour mixture. Be careful not to overmix. Remove the bowl from the stand and use a spatula to gently fold in any pockets of butter or flour.

3. Tip the dough onto a counter (no need to flour it) and, using the heel of your palm, push it together to form a 7-inch (18 cm) square. Wrap in plastic wrap and refrigerate for about 1 hour.

4. Meanwhile, preheat the oven to 350°F (180°C). Line two large sheet pans with parchment paper.

5. Unwrap the dough and place it between two sheets of parchment paper. Using a rolling pin, roll out the dough to about ⅜ inch (9 mm) thick. Place on one of the prepared pans, cover with plastic wrap, and refrigerate for another 15 minutes to chill the dough and prevent the cookies from spreading too much.

6. Using a 3-inch (8 cm) fluted cookie cutter or a thin drinking glass, cut out six rounds and place on the second prepared pan in three rows of two cookies. Gather the scraps, form them into another square, wrap in plastic wrap, and refrigerate for 15–20 minutes while you bake the first batch.

7. Using your fingertip, gently make a shallow divot in the center of each cookie. Place ½ teaspoon of the raspberry jam in each divot.

continued →

10. Using a small offset spatula, a knife, or a piping bag with a 10 mm star tip, spread about 1 tablespoon of the frosting on the flat side of a cookie. Place another cookie on top, flat side down, pressing gently to ensure the sandwich sticks together. Repeat to make eighteen sandwich cookies. Let set in the fridge for about 30–60 minutes before serving.

These cookies will keep in an airtight container in the fridge for up to 3 days or in the freezer for up to 2 months.

KITCHEN NOTES:

1. I detest using artificial ingredients such as food coloring; my one exception is for red velvet. I've tried using natural colorings, such as dehydrated beet or raspberry powder, but I keep coming back to food coloring for this one. I use Liqua-Gel food coloring by Chefmaster, which is good quality, with a fairly thick consistency. A cheap, runny food coloring may affect the consistency of the cookies. If you're against using any coloring at all, leave it out! The cookies will still be delicious.

2. To take these cookies to the next level, you can pipe a little raspberry jam in the center of the cream cheese before sandwiching the two cookies together.

3. Before baking, you can freeze the dough balls on the sheet pan, then transfer them to a freezer bag, squeezing out as much air as possible, and store in the freezer for up to 1 month. Thaw at room temperature for about 20 minutes, then bake.

Tom Tams

MAKES 12 SANDWICH COOKIES

1 recipe Chocolate Pastry
(page 236), cold

½ recipe Whipped Chocolate
Ganache (page 244;
see note)

1½ cups (260 g) dark
chocolate melts or wafers,
such as Ghirardelli
(see note)

My dad always had a stash of treats that he would hide from us kids—which we would inevitably find, often on top of the fridge! Tim Tams, a traditional Australian cookie, were one of my favorites among his stash. When we did get our hands on them, we would bite the end off and dip them in our cocoa. The whole thing would start to melt and crumble, and we'd have to stuff them in our mouths quickly to keep from wearing them, a refined technique known as the Tim Tam Slam. Although you can find Tim Tams in North American specialty stores or delicatessens, this is my version, homemade with pure ingredients.

1. Line two large sheet pans with parchment paper.

2. Let the pastry sit at room temperature for 5–10 minutes, well wrapped.

3. Cut the pastry in half and keep one half wrapped on the counter while you work with the other half.

4. On a lightly floured surface (see note), roll out the pastry into a 6 × 12-inch (15 × 30 cm) rectangle, just under ¼ inch (6 mm) thick. Make sure it is rolled evenly so it bakes evenly. Using a ruler and a knife, cut the pastry into twelve neat rectangles, each 1½ × 4 inches (4 × 10 cm). Dust off any excess flour.

5. Transfer the pastry rectangles onto one of the prepared pans, in neat rows (three rows of four works well), leaving about ½ inch (1.2 cm) between cookies. Using a fork, prick the pastry five or six times to prevent air pockets as it bakes.

6. Repeat steps 4 and 5 with the other half of the pastry. Cover and refrigerate for at least 15 minutes.

7. Meanwhile, preheat the oven to 350°F (180°C).

8. Bake, one pan at a time, for 10–14 minutes, rotating the pan after 6 minutes, or until the cookies no longer appear raw in the middle or undercooked. Let cool on the pan for 5 minutes, then transfer the cookies to a wire rack to cool completely.

9. Using a small offset spatula or palette knife, spread about 1 tablespoon of the ganache on the flat side of a cookie. Place another cookie on top, flat side down, pressing gently until the filling reaches the outer edges of the cookies. Repeat to make twelve sandwich cookies. Place them on a parchment-lined pan and refrigerate for 10–15 minutes or until the filling has completely set.

continued →

10. Meanwhile, bring a medium pot with about 1 inch (2.5 cm) of water to a boil, then lower the heat to a simmer. Top with a stainless steel bowl that is just big enough to fit snugly on top of the pot without touching the water. Add the chocolate melts and stir gently with a spatula until silky smooth. (Alternatively, you can microwave the chocolate in a bowl for 20 seconds at a time, stirring well after each interval, for about 1 minute, until melted and smooth. With either method, be careful not to overheat it, or the chocolate will seize and won't be usable.)

11. Transfer the melted chocolate into a small glass and dip the top half of each cookie into the chocolate, carefully scraping off excess chocolate. Return the dipped cookies to the parchment-lined pan. Let set at room temperature, about 5–10 minutes, depending on the temperature in your kitchen.

These cookies will keep in an airtight container at room temperature for 3–4 days, in the fridge for up to 2 weeks, or in the freezer for up to 1 month.

KITCHEN NOTES:

1. If you want to take these to the next level, you can use half chocolate ganache and half prepared chocolate hazelnut spread for the filling. Sprinkle chopped toasted hazelnuts onto the chocolate after dipping the cookies. Or you can try filling these with your favorite ice cream! Freeze the filled cookies, then dip halfway in melted chocolate and refreeze until you're ready to devour them!

2. This recipe uses a compound or coating chocolate for the cookie dip. You can use melted baking chocolate instead, but it may be a bit softer at room temperature.

3. You can use cocoa powder instead of flour to dust your surface, so you don't have white streaks on your chocolate dough, but it's a bit harder to clean up!

Orange, Hazelnut, and Chocolate Biscotti

1¾ cups (260 g) all-purpose flour

½ cup (50 g) cocoa powder

1 tsp baking powder

½ tsp baking soda

1 cup (200 g) granulated sugar

¼ cup (60 g) unsalted butter, softened

1 tsp pure vanilla extract

2½ tsp finely grated orange zest, divided

4 eggs, at room temperature, divided

1 cup (135 g) toasted whole hazelnuts, skins removed (see note)

2 Tbsp (25 g) coarse sugar (see note)

When I was traveling through Europe in my twenties, I once missed a connecting train and ended up in who-knows-where, Italy. I knocked on the door of a youth hostel, only to learn that while there were no rooms available inside, there was an abandoned building next door that I was welcome to crash in. I was greeted with missing floorboards, slashed mattresses, and an eerie essence hovering throughout the space. I dangled a flashlight from an old nail, unrolled my sleeping bag, and had one of the best sleeps of my life. The next morning, I was telling a bunch of newly arrived backpackers at the hostel about my adventure. That night, they all decided to join me, resulting in one giant, epic, days-long party. With limited funds, we survived happily on a diet of the contents of our flasks and biscotti from a nearby café, munching on these perfect, long-lasting morsels of sustenance.

1. Using a fine-mesh sieve, sift the flour, cocoa, baking powder, and baking soda into a small bowl.

2. In a stand mixer, combine the sugar, butter, vanilla, and 2 teaspoons of the orange zest. Using the paddle attachment, beat on medium speed until light and fluffy, about 1 minute. Add three of the eggs, one at a time, mixing on medium speed for about 10 seconds in between each egg, until well combined. Scrape down the bowl to ensure all the butter is fully incorporated. Add the flour mixture and mix on low speed until well combined, 15–20 seconds.

3. Remove the bowl from the stand and gently fold in the hazelnuts. Cover with a clean tea towel and let rest at room temperature for 1 hour.

4. Meanwhile, preheat the oven to 350°F (180°C) and position the oven racks in the upper and lower thirds of the oven. Line two large sheet pans with parchment paper.

5. Tip the dough onto a lightly floured surface and divide it in half. Shape each half into a log about 12 inches (30 cm) long. Place each log on a prepared pan.

6. Whisk the remaining egg with 1 tablespoon water and brush the mixture over both logs.

7. Mix the coarse sugar with the remaining orange zest. Sprinkle generously over the logs.

continued →

8. Bake for 30–40 minutes, rotating the pans after 15 minutes and swapping their positions in the oven, until the logs are golden brown and firm to the touch. Remove from the oven and lower the oven temperature to 200°F (100°C). Let the logs cool for about 15 minutes, then transfer to a cutting board and use a serrated knife to cut each log diagonally into ½-inch (1.2 cm) slices. You should get about twenty slices per log.

9. Return the pieces to the lined pans and bake for 30–40 minutes, flipping them over after 15 minutes, until dry and crisp. Let cool completely. Serve with hot chocolate, coffee, or Frangelico!

These biscotti will keep in an airtight container at room temperature for up to 4 weeks or in the freezer for up to 2 months.

KITCHEN NOTES:

1. To toast hazelnuts: Preheat the oven to 350°F (180°C). Line a rimmed sheet pan with parchment paper and spread nuts on it in a single layer. Toast for 10-15 minutes, tossing occasionally, until fragrant and starting to brown. Hazelnuts can go from toasted to burnt in seconds, so keep an eye on them! The skins should start to loosen when they are done. If you need to remove the skins, wrap the warm nuts in a clean dish towel and rub the towel roughly back and forth between your palms. The skins should crumble and fall right off. If your recipe calls for chopped nuts, let them cool completely before chopping.

2. If you don't have any coarse sugar, simply put 2 Tbsp (25 g) granulated sugar in a small mixing bowl and spritz with a little water. Mix the sugar around with a spoon until clumps form. Transfer it onto parchment paper and let it dry out. It will be crumbly and will have a great texture for topping the biscotti.

3. For extra pizzazz, these biscotti are fantastic when dipped diagonally into melted white chocolate, then sprinkled with crushed toasted hazelnuts and finely sliced candied orange peel.

Cranberry, Lemon, and Pistachio Biscotti

2¼ cups (335 g) all-purpose flour

1 tsp baking powder

½ tsp baking soda

1 cup (200 g) granulated sugar

¼ cup (60 g) unsalted butter, softened

2 tsp finely grated lemon zest, divided

1 tsp pure vanilla extract

4 eggs, at room temperature, divided

½ cup (70 g) sweetened dried cranberries

½ cup (80 g) whole raw pistachios

2 Tbsp (25 g) coarse sugar

When I was in grade seven, my mum and her dear friend discovered that both their kids had a growing love of baking. So one afternoon they got us together in the kitchen, equipped with bowls and whisks and a pile of sweet ingredients. We sifted and mixed, folded and blended, and together, we created some incredible confections, such as lollipops, marshmallows, toffee, cookies, honeycomb, and, of course, biscotti. Being the pros we so clearly were, we neatly packaged up our goods, took them to the local fair, sold out of everything, and made about $500 each! I may go so far as to say that this was the first step in my entrepreneurial journey to becoming a baker!

1. Using a fine-mesh sieve, sift the flour, baking powder, and baking soda into a small bowl.

2. In a stand mixer, combine the sugar, butter, 1 teaspoon of the lemon zest, and the vanilla. Using the paddle attachment, beat on medium speed until light and fluffy, about 1 minute. Add three of the eggs, one at a time, mixing on medium speed for about 10 seconds in between each egg, until well combined. Scrape down the bowl to ensure all the butter is fully incorporated. Add the flour mixture and mix on low speed until well combined, 15–20 seconds. Mix in the cranberries and pistachios, being careful not to overmix. Cover the bowl with a clean tea towel and let rest at room temperature for 1 hour.

3. Meanwhile, preheat the oven to 350°F (180°C) and position the oven racks in the upper and lower thirds of the oven. Line two large sheet pans with parchment paper.

4. Tip the dough onto a lightly floured surface and divide it in half. Shape each half into a log about 12 inches (30 cm) long. Place each log on a prepared pan.

5. Whisk the remaining egg with 1 tablespoon water and brush the mixture over both logs. Mix the coarse sugar with the remaining lemon zest. Sprinkle generously over the logs.

6. Bake for 30–40 minutes, rotating the pans after 15 minutes and swapping their positions in the oven, until the logs are golden brown and firm to the touch. Remove from the oven and lower the oven temperature to 200°F (100°C). Let the logs cool for about 15 minutes, then transfer to a cutting board and use a serrated knife to cut each log diagonally into ½-inch (1.2 cm) slices. You should get about twenty slices per log.

7. Return the pieces to the lined pans and bake for 30–40 minutes, flipping them over after 15 minutes, until dry and crisp. Transfer the biscotti to a wire rack and let cool completely.

These biscotti will keep in an airtight container at room temperature for up to 4 weeks or in the freezer for up to 2 months.

Gingerbread Walnut Biscotti

2 cups (300 g) all-purpose flour

1 Tbsp ground ginger

1 tsp baking powder

1 tsp ground cinnamon

½ tsp baking soda

½ tsp ground allspice

¼ tsp ground cloves

⅛ tsp ground white pepper

½ cup (100 g) granulated sugar

½ cup (100 g) dark brown sugar, lightly packed

¼ cup (60 g) unsalted butter, softened

1 Tbsp fancy molasses

1 tsp pure vanilla extract

4 eggs, at room temperature, divided

1 cup (140 g) chopped walnuts

½ cup (60 g) candied ginger, chopped into ¼-inch (6 mm) pieces

2 Tbsp (25 g) coarse sugar

Biscotti are great for more than just dipping in coffee. Serve them alongside a bowl of vanilla bean ice cream! Use them to make your own version of s'mores! Serve them with an iced or hot chai latte! Crumble them on top of an affogato! Or even sub them in for ladyfingers in a twist on trifle! Use your imagination, even icing the ends and dipping them in chopped candied ginger or chocolate. I encourage you to make these simple cookies your own!

1. Using a fine-mesh sieve, sift the flour, ground ginger, baking powder, cinnamon, baking soda, allspice, cloves, and pepper into a small bowl.

2. In a stand mixer, combine the granulated sugar, brown sugar, butter, molasses, and vanilla. Using the paddle attachment, beat on medium speed until light and fluffy, about 1 minute. Add three of the eggs, one at a time, mixing on medium speed for about 10 seconds in between each egg, until well combined. Scrape down the bowl to ensure all the butter is fully incorporated. Add the flour mixture and mix on low speed until well combined, 15–20 seconds. Gently mix in the walnuts and candied ginger.

3. Cover the bowl with a clean tea towel and let rest at room temperature for 1 hour.

4. Meanwhile, preheat the oven to 350°F (180°C) and position the oven racks in the upper and lower thirds of the oven. Line two large sheet pans with parchment paper.

5. Tip the dough onto a lightly floured surface and divide it in half. Shape each half into a log about 12 inches (30 cm) long. Place each log on a prepared pan.

6. Whisk the remaining egg with 1 tablespoon water and brush the mixture over both logs. Sprinkle each log generously with coarse sugar.

7. Bake for 30–40 minutes, rotating the pans after 15 minutes and swapping their positions in the oven, until the logs are golden brown and firm to the touch. Remove from the oven and lower the oven temperature to 200°F (100°C). Let the logs cool for about 15 minutes, then transfer to a cutting board and use a serrated knife to cut each log diagonally into ½-inch (1.2 cm) slices. You should get about twenty slices per log.

8. Return the pieces to the lined pans and bake for 30–40 minutes, flipping them over after 15 minutes, until dry and crisp. Transfer the biscotti to a wire rack and let cool completely. Serve with hot chocolate, coffee, or Madeira!

These biscotti will keep in an airtight container at room temperature for up to 4 weeks or in the freezer for up to 2 months.

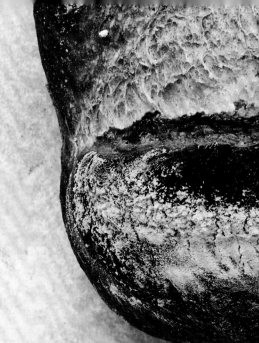

Breads

"The smell of good bread baking, like the sound
of lightly flowing water, is indescribable in
its evocation of innocence and delight."

M.F.K. FISHER

"Meet Yanni"

Sourdough Starter

Meet Yanni! This is what we have named our sourdough starter at Crust, as it is a bit of a baker's tradition to name the sourdough. (My starter in Australia was named Graham. Sadly, I could not smuggle Graham through customs.) I named Yanni after a dear friend, Ian, who was a long-term employee at Knead, my bakery in Australia. For reasons I cannot recall, Ian's nickname became Yanni. When I first moved to Canada and opened Crust, it made me long for my Australian colleagues and the beautiful relationships we had created at Knead. To bring a little piece of that to Crust, I named our starter Yanni, in honor of Ian, who was a hell of a bread maker!

Sourdough is a process, and with an incredible amount of information out in the world—and with a huge variance of methods and theories and sworn-by procedures—it can be overwhelming and can quickly become frustrating. Don't forget that this is just bread, and we're having fun with it! Over time, your baking intuition will get better, and you will focus less on the science of it all. Be patient as you find your own methods; as with all things, it takes some practice to master bread-making.

Expect it to take a week or so for the starter to get going, and about two weeks before you can make your first loaf. The starter will continue to gain more of a sour taste as time goes on. The ferment will keep forever if you treat it well and look after it, and the effort is worth it. Most importantly, don't forget to give it a name!

DAY 1

2 Tbsp (20 g) organic rye flour

½ cup (75 g) organic bread flour (see page 12)

½ tsp local, organic, raw, unprocessed honey

⅓ cup + 2 Tbsp (100 g) water, boiled and cooled to 85°F (30°C)

1. Wash your hands well and make sure all your bowls and mixing tools are very clean and dry. In a large glass or ceramic mixing bowl, combine the rye flour, bread flour, honey, and water. Using a large spatula, mix until you have a wet-looking dough. Be sure to scrape down the sides of the bowl to incorporate everything. Some lumps are fine.

2. Cover tightly with plastic wrap. Poke a few holes in the plastic to let gas escape, then cover with an upside-down plate. (Fruit flies love fermentation! The plate helps to keep them out.)

3. Leave the starter in a warm place (about 74°F/23°C) without touching it for 3 days. The dough will loosen up, smell a bit like alcohol or yeast, and start to look a little bubbly. This means fermentation has begun.

DAY 4

½ cup + 2 Tbsp (140 g) water, boiled and cooled to 85°F (30°C)

1 cup (150 g) organic bread flour

1. Using a large spatula, mix the water into the fermented mixture, then add the flour. Again, mix until you have a wet dough, being sure to scrape down the sides of the bowl to incorporate everything. Some lumps are fine.

2. Leave in the same warm spot, covered, for another 2 days.

continued →

→ Sprouted Four-Seed Sourdough (page 182) ↑ Matt's Camp Oven Sourdough 101 (page 177)

Sprouted Four-Seed Sourdough

Sprouted Seeds

¼ cup (35 g) flax seeds

¼ cup (35 g) pumpkin seeds

¼ cup (35 g) sesame seeds

¼ cup (35 g) sunflower seeds

Dough

2½ cups (375 g) bread flour (see page 12)

1¾ cups (260 g) whole wheat flour

1½ cups (375 ml) water, boiled and cooled to 85°F (30°C)

1¼ cups (340 g) sourdough starter, at room temperature (see page 173)

1 Tbsp kosher salt

Flour for sprinkling (optional; any kind will do)

I wanted to introduce a seedy bread to the Crust repertoire but found that most breads with toasted seeds were a bit hard on the teeth! Soaking and slightly sprouting the seeds not only softens them a bit but also adds a layer of healthfulness to the loaf. While we have never claimed Crust to be a health food bakery (by any means!), I am happy this bread quickly became popular in the midst of our vast array of pastries and cakes. A spread of avocado and sprouts with fresh tomatoes, cucumbers, and a generous grind of black pepper is lovely on this bread, but I would not judge you for stuffing it with cream cheese and lox!

1. **SPROUT THE SEEDS:** The day before starting the bread, combine all four seeds in a small sealable container and cover with ½ cup (125 ml) cold water. Refrigerate, covered, for up to 24 hours (no longer, or they will start to sprout too much; you want to catch them at the very beginning of sprouting).

2. **MAKE THE DOUGH:** In a stand mixer, combine the bread flour, whole wheat flour, water, starter, and salt. Using the dough hook attachment, mix on low speed for 2 minutes or until thoroughly combined. (Or mix with your hands in a large mixing bowl.)

3. Increase the mixer speed to medium-high and knead for 5–7 minutes or until the dough is pulling away from the bowl and starts to become cohesive. (If kneading by hand, knead the dough on a lightly floured surface for at least 10 minutes and up to 30 minutes, depending on the type of flour you're using.) The finished dough should be just a bit tacky (not sticky), should look smooth and silky, and should pass the window test (see note on page 179).

4. Discard any excess water from the seeds. Add the seeds to the dough and knead for 1 minute to combine.

5. Spray or brush a large piece of parchment paper with a neutral oil. Set the paper in a large bowl, oil side up.

6. Using your thumbs and the heels of both hands, pull the dough taut from the top as you wobble and tuck it underneath itself to the bottom, forming a ball with a top that is tight and smooth. Place the dough on the oiled paper in the bowl, cover the bowl with plastic wrap, and set it in a warm place (see notes on page 179) for 2 hours to proof. The dough should double in size.

7. Turn the dough out onto a clean counter. Gently flatten and stretch it out into a square about 7 inches (18 cm) across. Fold each corner into the center to create a smaller square. It's okay to trap small pockets of air at this stage. Wobble and tuck the dough into a ball with a taut and smooth top, as in step 6. Return the dough to the parchment-lined bowl, smooth side up, and cover with plastic wrap. Refrigerate for 8–24 hours, depending on how much lactic/acetic acid (sourness) you want to build up in the bread. The longer it sits, the sourer it will get, though you don't want to leave it for much more than 24 hours, as the yeast will no longer be active and the loaf will end up flat and lifeless.

8. When you are ready to bake, remove the bowl from the fridge and set it in your warm proofing spot, still covered, for 30–60 minutes or until the dough is tripled in size.

9. Meanwhile, place a covered 5- to 7-quart cast-iron Dutch oven on the middle rack of the cold oven, set the heat to 430°F (220°C), and leave for 35 minutes. Gather a spray bottle of water, flour for sprinkling (if using), and a bread lame or small serrated knife lightly sprayed with a neutral oil.

10. Once the pot is very hot, do the following in quick succession: Carefully remove the pot from the oven and remove the lid. (I recommend leaving your oven mitt on top of the lid so you are not tempted to grab it with your bare hand!) Lift the dough ball out of the bowl, holding it by the paper, and place it carefully in the hot pot. Generously spray the top of the loaf with water to help create steam for the lovely, glossy, bubbly crust. If desired, sprinkle some flour over the top of the loaf for decoration.

11. Using the lame, make two cuts, about 1 inch (2.5 cm) deep, in the top of the loaf where you want it to "burst." Try to make each slash in one smooth motion.

12. Replace the lid and return the pot to the oven. Bake for 30 minutes, then remove the lid and bake for 10–20 minutes or until the loaf is deep golden brown, and darker along the edges of the cut. Grasping the paper, lift the loaf out onto a wire rack. It should sound hollow when tapped on the bottom. If it doesn't, return it to the oven for another 5–10 minutes. Let cool on the rack for at least 30 minutes (see note on page 179).

This bread will keep in a sealed plastic, paper, or linen bag at room temperature for up to 3 days or in the freezer for up to 3 months. I don't recommend refrigerating it.

Potato, Asiago, and Green Onion Sourdough

MAKES 1 LOAF

Potatoes

5 oz (150 g) white or Yukon
Gold potatoes (unpeeled),
cut into ¾-inch (2 cm)
cubes

1 Tbsp extra virgin
olive oil

1½ tsp kosher salt

½ tsp freshly cracked
black pepper

2 tsp bread flour

Dough

4¼ cups (640 g) bread
flour (see page 12)

1½ cups (375 ml) water,
boiled and cooled to 85°F
(30°C)

1¼ cups (340 g) sourdough
starter, at room temperature
(see page 173)

1 Tbsp kosher salt

½ cup (50 g) finely grated
Asiago or Parmesan cheese,
divided

2 Tbsp (20 g) finely sliced
green onions

2 tsp freshly cracked
black pepper

Flour for sprinkling
(optional; any kind
will do)

When I need something new at Crust, I gather my staff for a brainstorming session over coffee and sweets. I knew I wanted a potato loaf of some kind for an upcoming fall and winter menu, and after tossing around ideas for a while, we came up with the idea of leaving potato chunks, skin and all, in the loaf and adding green onions and cheese to complement them. Sort of like a baked potato in bread form! It's fantastic to set in front of a group of guests, along with a pot of beef stew, and allow friends to slice pieces for themselves. Topped with fresh summer tomatoes, a slice of this bread is both bright and earthy. Thinly sliced, toasted, and swiped through a bowl of homemade hummus, it is an ideal last-minute hors d'oeuvre.

1. **MAKE THE POTATOES:** Preheat the oven to 400°F (200°C).

2. In a small ovenproof dish, toss the potatoes with the oil, salt, and pepper. Cover with foil.

3. Bake for 15 minutes. Let cool to room temperature and refrigerate for up to 2 days.

4. **MAKE THE DOUGH:** In a stand mixer, combine the flour, water, starter, and salt. Using the dough hook attachment, mix on low speed for 2 minutes or until thoroughly combined. (Or mix with your hands in a large mixer bowl.)

5. Increase the mixer speed to medium-high and knead for 5–7 minutes or until the dough is pulling away from the bowl and starts to become cohesive. (If kneading by hand, knead the dough on a lightly floured surface for at least 10 minutes and up to 30 minutes, depending on the type of flour you're using.) In the last minute of kneading, add most of the Asiago, reserving about 1 tablespoon, then add the green onions and pepper, distributing them evenly throughout the dough. The finished dough should be just a bit tacky (not sticky), should look smooth and silky, and should pass the window test (see note on page 179).

6. Spray or brush a large piece of parchment paper with a neutral oil. Set the paper in a large bowl, oil side up.

7. Using your thumbs and the heels of both hands, pull the dough taut from the top as you wobble and tuck it underneath itself to the bottom, forming a ball with a top that is tight and smooth. Place the dough on the oiled paper in the bowl, cover the bowl with plastic wrap, and set it in a warm place (see notes on page 179) for 2 hours to proof. The dough should double in size.

continued →

8. Turn the dough out onto a clean counter. Gently flatten and stretch it out into a square about 7 inches (18 cm) across. Toss the potatoes in 2 teaspoons bread flour, then evenly scatter them over the dough. Fold each corner into the center to create a smaller square. It's okay to trap small pockets of air at this stage. Wobble and tuck the dough into a ball with a taut and smooth top, as in step 7. Return the dough to the parchment-lined bowl, smooth side up, and cover with plastic wrap. Refrigerate for 8–24 hours, depending on how much lactic/acetic acid (sourness) you want to build up in the bread. The longer it sits, the sourer it will get, though you don't want to leave it for much more than 24 hours, as the yeast will no longer be active and the loaf will end up flat and lifeless.

9. When you are ready to bake, remove the bowl from the fridge and set it in your warm proofing spot, still covered, for 30–60 minutes or until the dough is tripled in size.

10. Meanwhile, place a covered 5- to 7-quart cast-iron Dutch oven on the middle rack of the cold oven, set the heat to 430°F (220°C), and leave for 35 minutes. Gather a spray bottle of water, flour for sprinkling (if using), and a bread lame or small serrated knife lightly sprayed with a neutral oil.

11. Once the pot is very hot, do the following in quick succession: Carefully remove the pot from the oven and remove the lid. (I recommend leaving your oven mitt on top of the lid so you are not tempted to grab it with your bare hand!) Lift the dough ball out of the bowl, holding it by the paper, and place it carefully in the hot pot. Generously spray the top of the loaf with water to help create steam for the lovely, glossy, bubbly crust. If desired, sprinkle some flour over the top of the loaf for decoration. Sprinkle the remaining Asiago over the top of the loaf.

12. Using the lame, make a long cut, about 1 inch (2.5 cm) deep, in the center on top of the loaf, where you want it to "burst." Try to slash the dough in one smooth motion.

13. Replace the lid and return the pot to the oven. Bake for 30 minutes, then remove the lid and bake for 10–20 minutes or until the loaf is deep golden brown, and darker along the edges of the cut. Grasping the paper, lift the loaf out onto a wire rack. It should sound hollow when tapped on the bottom. If it doesn't, return it to the oven for another 5–10 minutes. Let cool on the rack for at least 30 minutes (see note on page 179).

    This bread will keep in a sealed plastic, paper, or linen bag at room temperature for 1–2 days or in the freezer for up to 3 months. I don't recommend refrigerating it, as the potatoes will turn gray.

Cranberry Walnut Sourdough

¼ cup (35 g) chopped
walnuts

2½ cups (375 g) bread
flour (see page 12)

1¾ cups (260 g) whole
wheat flour

1½ cups (375 ml) water,
boiled and cooled to 85°F
(30°C)

1¼ cups (340 g) sourdough
starter, at room
temperature (see page 173)

1 Tbsp kosher salt

¼ cup (35 g) unsweetened
dried cranberries

Flour for sprinkling
(optional; any kind
will do)

This bread is perfect for a turkey and Brie sandwich with crispy lettuce and a bit of mayo. With the cranberries baked right in, it is like a handheld Thanksgiving dinner! Toasted or not, it goes well with most cheeses, and is great for breakfast, slathered with butter or preserves. We make it seasonally at Crust, and our customers often buy two or three loaves—one to eat, one to freeze, and (maybe) one to share.

1. Preheat the oven to 375°F (190°C). Spread the walnuts out on a sheet pan and toast for 7–10 minutes or until golden brown. Let cool completely.

2. In a stand mixer, combine the bread flour, whole wheat flour, water, starter, and salt. Using the dough hook attachment, mix on low speed for 2 minutes or until thoroughly combined. (Or mix with your hands in a large mixing bowl.)

3. Increase the mixer speed to medium-high and knead for 5–7 minutes or until the dough is pulling away from the bowl and starts to become cohesive. (If kneading by hand, knead the dough on a lightly floured surface for at least 10 minutes and up to 30 minutes, depending on the type of flour you're using.) The finished dough should be just a bit tacky (not sticky), should look smooth and silky, and should pass the window test (see note on page 179). Add the cranberries and toasted walnuts and knead for 1 minute to combine.

4. Spray or brush a large piece of parchment paper with a neutral oil. Set the paper in a large bowl, oil side up.

5. Using your thumbs and the heels of both hands, pull the dough taut from the top as you wobble and tuck it underneath itself to the bottom, forming a ball with a top that is tight and smooth. Place the dough on the oiled paper in the bowl, cover the bowl with plastic wrap, and set it in a warm place (see notes on page 179) for 2 hours to proof. The dough should double in size.

6. Turn the dough out onto a clean counter. Gently flatten and stretch it out into a square about 7 inches (18 cm) across. Fold each corner into the center to create a smaller square. It's okay to trap small pockets of air at this stage. Wobble and tuck the dough into a ball with a taut and smooth top, as in step 5. Return the dough to the parchment-lined bowl, smooth side up, and cover with plastic wrap. Refrigerate for 8–24 hours, depending on how much lactic/acetic acid (sourness) you want to build up in the bread. The longer it sits, the sourer it will get, though you don't want to leave it for much more than 24 hours, as the yeast will no longer be active and the loaf will end up flat and lifeless.

7. When you are ready to bake, remove the bowl from the fridge and set it in your warm proofing spot, still covered, for 30–60 minutes or until the dough is tripled in size.

continued →

8. Meanwhile, place a covered 5- to 7-quart cast-iron Dutch oven on the middle rack of the cold oven, set the heat to 430°F (220°C), and leave for 35 minutes. Gather a spray bottle of water, flour for sprinkling (if using), and a bread lame or small serrated knife lightly sprayed with a neutral oil.

9. Once the pot is very hot, do the following in quick succession: Carefully remove the pot from the oven and remove the lid. (I recommend leaving your oven mitt on top of the lid so you are not tempted to grab it with your bare hand!) Lift the dough ball out of the bowl, holding it by the paper, and place it carefully in the hot pot. Generously spray the top of the loaf with water to help create steam for the lovely, glossy, bubbly crust. If desired, sprinkle some flour over the top of the loaf for decoration.

10. Using the lame, make four cuts, about 1 inch (2.5 cm) deep, in a square pattern in the center on top of the loaf, where you want it to "burst." Try to make each slash in one smooth motion.

11. Replace the lid and return the pot to the oven. Bake for 30 minutes, then remove the lid and bake for 10–20 minutes or until the loaf is deep golden brown, and darker along the edges of the cut. Grasping the paper, lift the loaf out onto a wire rack. It should sound hollow when tapped on the bottom. If it doesn't, return it to the oven for another 5–10 minutes. Let cool on the rack for at least 30 minutes (see note on page 179).

This bread will keep in a sealed plastic, paper, or linen bag at room temperature for up to 3 days or in the freezer for up to 3 months. I don't recommend refrigerating it.

1 whole star anise pod
(optional)

½ tsp finely grated
lemon zest

½ tsp kosher salt

¼ tsp freshly cracked
black pepper

6. Remove the lid, lower the heat to medium-low, and cook, stirring occasionally and allowing the liquid to evaporate as it cooks down, for about 30 minutes. When the liquid has almost entirely evaporated, remove the pan from the heat and discard the bay leaf and star anise. Let cool.

7. **FINISH THE BREAD:** Preheat the oven to 400°F (200°C). Brush two large rimmed sheet pans with extra virgin olive oil.

8. Tip the dough onto the clean counter and cut it evenly in half. Using your fingertips, gently stretch out each half into a 6 × 9-inch (15 × 23 cm) rectangle. If they spring back without keeping their shape, let them rest on the counter, lightly covered with plastic wrap, for a few minutes, then try again.

9. Place each rectangle on a prepared pan, cover with a clean, dry tea towel, and place in your warm spot until the dough has risen and puffed a bit, about 25 minutes. The dough should be about 1 inch (2.5 cm) thick. You will prepare and bake one loaf at a time (unless you have two ovens—lucky you!), so leave the second loaf in its warm spot until you are ready for it.

10. Using a spoon, spread half of the caramelized onion mixture, as well as half of the liquid from the pan, over the first loaf. Drizzle with half of the olive oil and sprinkle with half of the flaky salt. Now for the fun part! Using all ten fingertips, press them into the dough, all the way to the bottom. Repeat six times, evenly over the dough, to create little wells all over the surface. The loaf will spread out a bit, and that's just fine.

11. Bake for 15–20 minutes or until the focaccia is golden brown all over. Sprinkle half of the fresh thyme over top. Allow it to cool for 10 minutes on a wire rack before eating.

12. Repeat steps 10 and 11 with the second loaf.

This bread will keep in an airtight container or heavy-duty plastic bag at room temperature for up to 2 days, or in a well-sealed, airtight bag in the fridge for up to 4 days. Make sure the bag is airtight so your fridge doesn't end up smelling of onions! Because of the onions, I don't recommend freezing this loaf.

Feta, Oregano, and Lemon Focaccia

Bread

1¼ cups (300 ml) lukewarm water (90-100°F/32-38°C)

2¼ tsp instant dry yeast

3 cups (450 g) bread flour (see page 12)

2 Tbsp (30 ml) vegetable oil

2 tsp kosher salt

2 tsp granulated sugar

1 tsp honey

⅔ cup (100 g) crumbled feta cheese, divided

1 tsp flaky sea salt, divided

Topping

¼ cup (60 ml) extra virgin olive oil

2 cloves garlic, finely minced

½ cup (10 g) fresh oregano, roughly chopped (see note)

2 Tbsp (30 ml) fresh lemon juice

2 tsp roughly chopped preserved lemon rind (see note)

½ tsp dried red chili flakes

½ tsp freshly cracked black pepper

This recipe, with its combo of spicy oregano, garlic, and lemon, is an ode to my wife's Greek heritage. Speaking from experience, exercise caution if you are using homegrown oregano, as it can sometimes be overwhelmingly powerful. Taste it raw before mixing it into the topping and adjust the amount accordingly. My father-in-law grows a variety that is coveted by many friends and family members, as it has a mild, slightly spicy flavor, and that was the inspiration for this focaccia. He encourages us to use only the flowers and buds, rather than the leaves, which is a curious but beautiful option if you have it. Doing so makes it a little more flavorful and adds a touch of sweetness that pairs beautifully with the preserved lemon.

1. **START THE BREAD:** In a medium bowl, combine the water and yeast, stirring gently with a fork until the yeast is dissolved.

2. In a stand mixer, combine the flour, vegetable oil, kosher salt, sugar, and honey. Add the yeast mixture and stir to combine, scraping down the sides. Using the dough hook attachment, mix on low speed until all the ingredients are well combined, 30–60 seconds. Increase the speed to medium-high and mix for another 4–5 minutes, until a smooth dough has formed. Keep an eye on the dough: it should not be sticking to the sides or bottom of the bowl. If it is, decrease the speed and carefully add 1–2 teaspoons of flour.

3. Remove the dough from the bowl and lightly spray or brush the bowl with neutral oil. Return the dough to the bowl and cover loosely with plastic wrap. Set it in a warm place for 30 minutes to proof (see note on page 179). You won't see a lot of action here just yet; the dough is just getting started.

4. Place the dough on a lightly floured counter and gently stretch it a little, then fold it in half. Turn the dough ninety degrees and gently stretch it and fold in half again. Repeat twice more, so that you have folded the dough four times in total. Return the dough to the greased bowl, cover with the plastic wrap, and return it to your warm proofing spot for another 30–45 minutes or until the dough has risen and doubled in size.

5. Preheat the oven to 400°F (200°C). Brush two large rimmed sheet pans with extra virgin olive oil.

6. Tip the dough onto a clean counter (lightly floured) and cut it evenly in half. Using your fingertips, gently stretch out each half into a 6 × 9-inch (15 × 23 cm) rectangle. If they spring back without keeping their shape, let them rest on the counter, lightly covered with plastic wrap, for a few minutes, then try again.

continued →

7. Place each rectangle on a prepared pan, cover with a clean, dry tea towel, and place in your warm spot until the dough has risen and puffed a bit, about 25 minutes. The dough should be about 1 inch (2.5 cm) thick. You will prepare and bake one loaf at a time (unless you have two ovens—lucky you!), so leave the second loaf in its warm spot until you are ready for it.

8. **MAKE THE TOPPING:** In a small bowl, mix the olive oil, garlic, oregano, lemon juice, preserved lemon rind, chili flakes, and pepper until combined.

9. **FINISH THE BREAD:** Crumble half of the feta over the first loaf. Now for the fun part! Using all ten fingertips, press them into the dough, all the way to the bottom. Repeat six times, evenly over the dough, to create little wells all over the surface. The loaf will spread out a bit, and that's just fine. Drizzle half of the topping over the loaf and sprinkle with half of the flaky salt.

10. Bake for 15–20 minutes or until the focaccia is golden brown all over. Allow it to cool for 10 minutes on a wire rack before eating.

11. Repeat steps 9 and 10 with the second loaf.

    This bread will keep in an airtight container or heavy-duty plastic bag at room temperature for up to 2 days or in the fridge for up to 4 days, or in a well-sealed freezer bag for up to 2 months.

KITCHEN NOTES:

1. Oregano varies greatly in intensity. If you have a more medicinal-tasting fresh oregano, feel free to use less, or use 1 teaspoon of dried oregano and top up the measurement with fresh parsley.

2. If you don't have preserved lemon rind, replace it with 1 teaspoon finely grated lemon zest.

3. This dough freezes quite well, so you could freeze one half and bake the other right away. After step 2, tightly wrap the dough you'll be freezing in plastic wrap and store in an airtight container in the freezer for up to 2 weeks. Thaw overnight in the fridge, then go straight on to proofing in step 3.

Roasted Tomato and Green Olive Focaccia

Bread

1¼ cups (300 ml) lukewarm water (90–100°F/32–38°C)

2¼ tsp instant dry yeast

3 cups (450 g) bread flour (see page 12)

2 Tbsp (30 ml) vegetable oil

2 tsp kosher salt

2 tsp granulated sugar

1 tsp honey

½ cup (140 g) sliced green olives

¾ cup (16 g) flat-leaf parsley, coarsely chopped, divided

3 Tbsp (20 g) freshly grated Parmesan cheese, divided

Topping

2 cups (360 g) cherry tomatoes

3 Tbsp (45 ml) extra virgin olive oil

4 cloves garlic, thinly sliced

1 tsp fresh thyme leaves

2 tsp flaky sea salt, divided

½ tsp dried red chili flakes

¼ tsp freshly cracked black pepper

It could be said that when I first started gardening for my restaurant Grazing, in Gundaroo, I was very . . . enthusiastic. I planted eight beds of tomatoes and ended up with so many that I had to transport them to the walk-in cooler in wheelbarrows, where they sat as I pondered what to do with them! Let's just say there were a lot of roasted, sliced, sauced tomatoes on the menu that year. This is one of the recipes I came up with to use up some of the bounty. With olives and Parmesan, it is reminiscent of a delicious thick-crust pizza, full of herbs and olive oil and all those good earthly things. It goes without saying that this recipe benefits from using tomatoes that are at the peak of their season.

1. **START THE BREAD:** In a medium bowl, combine the water and yeast, stirring gently with a fork until the yeast is dissolved.

2. In a stand mixer, combine the flour, vegetable oil, kosher salt, sugar, and honey. Add the yeast mixture and stir to combine, scraping down the sides. Using the dough hook attachment, mix on low speed until all the ingredients are well combined, 30–60 seconds. Increase the speed to medium-high and mix for another 4–5 minutes. Keep an eye on the dough: it should not be sticking to the sides or bottom of the bowl. If it is, decrease the speed and carefully add 1–2 teaspoons of flour. Add the olives and 3 tablespoons (45 ml) of the parsley and mix for 20 seconds or until well incorporated through the dough.

3. Remove the dough from the bowl and lightly spray or brush the bowl with a neutral oil. Return the dough to the bowl and cover loosely with plastic wrap. Set it in a warm place for 30 minutes to proof (see note on page 179). You won't see a lot of action here just yet; the dough is just getting started.

4. Place the dough on a clean counter (no need to flour it) and gently stretch it a little, then fold it in half. Turn the dough ninety degrees and gently stretch it and fold in half again. Repeat twice more, so that you have folded the dough four times in total. Return the dough to the greased bowl, cover with the plastic wrap, and return it to your warm proofing spot for another 30–45 minutes or until the dough has risen and doubled in size.

5. Meanwhile, preheat the oven to 400°F (200°C). Brush two large rimmed sheet pans with extra virgin olive oil.

continued →

6. **MAKE THE TOPPING:** On a parchment-lined rimmed sheet pan, toss the tomatoes with the olive oil, garlic, thyme, 1 teaspoon of the flaky salt, and the chili flakes and pepper. Roast for 15–20 minutes or until the tomatoes have started to crack and the herbs and garlic are fragrant. Remove from the oven, leaving the oven on, and let cool.

7 **FINISH THE BREAD:** Tip the dough onto the clean counter and cut it evenly in half. Using your fingertips, gently stretch out each half into a 6 × 9-inch (15 × 23 cm) rectangle. If they spring back without keeping their shape, let them rest on the counter, lightly covered with plastic wrap, for a few minutes, then try again.

8. Place each rectangle on a prepared pan, cover with a clean, dry tea towel, and place in your warm spot until the dough has risen and puffed a bit, about 25 minutes. The dough should be about 1 inch (2.5 cm) thick. You will prepare and bake one loaf at a time (unless you have two ovens—lucky you!), so leave the second loaf in its warm spot until you are ready for it.

9. Now for the fun part! Using all ten fingertips, press them into the dough of the first loaf, all the way to the bottom. Repeat six times, evenly over the dough, to create little wells all over the surface. The loaf will spread out a bit, and that's just fine. Press half of the tomatoes firmly into some of the wells, evenly distributing them across the dough. Drizzle half of the olive oil pan juices over top.

10. Bake for 15–20 minutes or until the focaccia is golden brown all over. Immediately sprinkle with half of the Parmesan, half of the remaining parsley, and half of the remaining flaky salt. Allow it to cool for 10 minutes on a wire rack before eating.

11. Repeat steps 9 and 10 with the second loaf.

This bread will keep in an airtight container or heavy-duty plastic bag at room temperature for up to 2 days, or in a well-sealed, airtight bag in the fridge for up to 4 days. Make sure the bag is airtight so your fridge doesn't end up smelling of garlic! I don't recommend freezing this loaf.

Rustic Rye Bread

3⅓ cups (500 g) bread
flour (see page 12),
plus more as needed

⅓ cup (50 g) light rye
flour (see note)

1½ tsp kosher salt

1 tsp instant dry yeast

1⅔ cups (400 ml) water,
at room temperature

Back in 2000 in Canberra, I was recruited to help open a hybrid restaurant/bakery alongside a talented pastry chef. As we worked together to create this beautiful space and menu, we became great mates. He would work overnight, proofing and baking and prepping, and I would come in each morning, incorporating his baked goods into my daily restaurant menu. I was always completely blown away by what he could create in his tiny space. He was an absolute champ at all he did, and he taught me so much about baking and pastries. He kindly shared this rye recipe with me, and I've been using it faithfully ever since.

1. In a stand mixer, combine the bread flour, rye flour, salt, yeast, and water. Using the dough hook attachment, mix on low speed for about 20 seconds. Increase the speed to medium-high and mix for about 2 minutes until the ingredients come together. The dough should be a little sticky, but if you notice that it is sticking to the bottom of the bowl, add another 1–2 tablespoons of bread flour and mix again.

2. Tip the dough out onto a lightly floured surface and, using lightly floured hands, knead it, stretching and turning, for another 5 minutes. The finished dough should be just a bit tacky (not sticky), should look smooth and silky, and should pass the window test (see note on page 179).

3. Lightly brush or spray the mixer bowl with a neutral oil and return the dough to the bowl. Cover with plastic wrap and set in a warm place (see notes on page 179) for 90 minutes or until the dough has doubled in size.

4. Line a large sheet pan with parchment paper. Tip the dough out onto a lightly floured surface and, using lightly floured hands, gently flatten it into an 8 × 15-inch (20 × 38 cm) rectangle, about 1 inch (2.5 cm) thick. Don't press too hard when you are flattening it: you just want to knock out the large air pockets while leaving the smaller air pockets intact.

5. Lightly reflour the counter if needed, then lay the dough with a long side toward you. Fold the dough from the left side into the center, then repeat with the right side to form a square. Gently press the dough down, using your fingertips to help it stay in place. Starting with the edge farthest away from you, gently roll the dough loosely toward you, like a jelly roll. Pinch along the seam to seal the dough into a loaf; it should look like a fat, smooth log. Roll the loaf back and forth on the counter to make it a little longer—about 10 inches (25 cm).

6. Place the loaf, seam side down, on the prepared pan. Cover the loaf with lightly oiled plastic wrap and place the pan in your warm proofing spot for another 60–90 minutes or until the dough has doubled in size.

continued →

7. Preheat the oven to 440°F (227°C), with one rack in the middle and one in the lower third. Place a rimmed sheet pan on the lower rack to use as a steam tray. Put a kettle of water on to boil.

8. If desired, sprinkle the loaf with a little extra flour and make patterns in it with your fingers.

9. When you're ready to bake, move quickly; otherwise, your dough may fall apart. Using a bread lame or serrated knife, make a 2-inch (5 cm) deep cut from one end of the loaf to the other, in the top center. Try to slash the dough in one smooth motion. Place the sheet pan with the loaf on the middle rack of the oven and quickly pour about 1 cup (250 ml) of boiled water into the steam tray on the lower rack. Be very careful, as the water will steam aggressively! Lower the temperature to 400°F (200°C).

10. Bake for 35–45 minutes, rotating the pan after 20 minutes to ensure even baking, until the loaf is a deep golden brown all over and the bottom sounds hollow when tapped. Let cool completely on a wire rack before slicing.

This bread will keep in a sealed plastic, paper, or linen bag at room temperature for up to 2 days. It also freezes well; the secret is to slice it first, then place the slices in a freezer bag and freeze for up to 3 months. At home, I toast it straight from frozen.

KITCHEN NOTE:

1. In this recipe, in which I use light (also called white) rye flour, rye makes up only about 10% of the flour. I find this ratio gives the bread a lovely flavor without being too earthy or heavy. However, feel free to experiment with different types of rye flour to get different results.

Aussie Crunch Buns

Bread

4⅓ cups (640 g) all-purpose flour

3 Tbsp (37 g) granulated sugar

1 Tbsp kosher salt

6 Tbsp (93 g) Philadelphia-style cream cheese

2 Tbsp (30 g) unsalted butter, at room temperature

2¼ tsp instant dry yeast

1⅓ cups (325 ml) lukewarm water (90-100°F/32-38°C)

1 egg, at room temperature

Topping

1¼ cups (200 g) rice flour (see note)

3 Tbsp (37 g) granulated sugar

2¼ tsp instant dry yeast

2 tsp kosher salt

¾ cup + 2 Tbsp (205 ml) lukewarm water (90-100°F/32-38°C)

⅓ cup (75 ml) vegetable oil

These buns are also called Dutch crunch buns—or tiger buns, due to their stripy appearance. By whatever name, they all have that signature crackle on top, making them a delicious vessel for softer foods such as avocado and cheese. Or try making a sandwich with roasted chicken, sweet chili sauce, cilantro, mayo, and fresh lettuce. While I find all of these options appealing, in true Aussie fashion, my favorite way to eat these buns is with a simple smear of butter and Vegemite!

1. **MAKE THE BREAD:** In a stand mixer, stir together the flour, sugar, salt, cream cheese, butter, and yeast. Add the water and egg. Using the dough hook attachment, mix on low speed until a rough-looking dough forms, about 1 minute.

2. Increase the mixer speed to medium and mix until the dough looks smooth, about 15 minutes. The dough should not stick to the bottom of the bowl during this process; instead, it should "clean" the sides of the bowl as it mixes, pulling away from the sides into a cohesive ball. If it seems too sticky, add 1 teaspoon of flour. If it seems too dry and isn't coming together, add 1 teaspoon of water. It is better to err on the sticky side, as you can adjust by adding more flour during kneading. It is harder to add water once the dough comes together. Stop the mixer several times throughout the mixing process to scrape the dough off the dough hook, if needed.

3. Remove the dough from the bowl and knead it lightly into a smooth, round ball. Lightly grease the bowl, then return the dough to the bowl. Cover with plastic wrap and set in a warm place (see note on page 179) for 1 hour. The dough should double in size.

4. Line two large sheet pans with parchment paper. Tip the dough onto a lightly floured surface. Using lightly floured fingertips, gently press it into a 10 × 14-inch (25 × 35 cm) rectangle, about 1 inch (2.5 cm) thick. Using a pastry scraper or dull knife, cut the dough in half lengthwise, then cut each half into six equal pieces. Firmly flatten out each piece, one at a time, to form a 3 × 5-inch (8 × 13 cm) rectangle.

5. Working with one rectangle at a time, lay it with a long side toward you. Starting with the side farthest from you, carefully fold over one-third of the dough. Using the heel of your hand, lightly tap down on the folded dough to remove any air bubbles. Starting at the back again, fold it in half to form a 1-inch (2.5 cm) wide cylinder. Pinch along the seam to seal the dough. Lightly roll the cylinder back and forth on the counter to ensure the seam is sealed and to make it a little longer—about 6 inches (15 cm). Repeat to make twelve buns.

continued →

6. Place six buns, seam side down, in two rows of three on each prepared pan, leaving as much space as possible in between. Cover the buns loosely with lightly oiled plastic wrap and place the pans in your warm proofing spot for 40–50 minutes or until the buns are one and a half times their original size and are slightly springy when poked with a finger.

7. Preheat the oven to 400°F (200°C), with one rack in the top third and one in the lower third or middle.

8. **MAKE THE TOPPING:** In a medium bowl, stir together the rice flour, sugar, yeast, and salt. Add the water and oil and whisk together to get a smooth paste. Cover with plastic wrap and let rest at room temperature for 20 minutes before using.

9. This next part is a little messy and should be done only when the buns are ready to go in the oven. Using a small offset spatula, spread 1 tablespoon of the topping over each bun. Don't worry if the topping falls off a bit, so long as there is a thin, even amount covering each bun.

10. Place both pans in the oven and close the door, working quickly so you don't lose too much heat. Lower the temperature to 350°F (180°C). Bake for 24–28 minutes, rotating the trays after 12 minutes to ensure even baking, until the buns are deep golden brown all over and the tops have a crackle effect. Transfer the buns to a wire rack and let cool completely before serving.

    These buns will keep in an airtight container at room temperature for 3 days or in the freezer for up to 1 month.

KITCHEN NOTES:

1. Rice flour is simply finely ground white rice. It can be purchased at most grocery stores, or you can make it yourself by grinding 1 cup (200 g) of white rice in a flour mill or spice grinder and sifting it through a fine-mesh sieve. Since rice and grinders can vary, be sure to measure the rice flour once it's processed.

2. When rolling the buns, be quick and try not to handle the dough too much or you will melt the butter and the dough will become glossy and sticky, making it difficult to shape properly. A little sprinkle of flour might help, but ideally, ask someone with cool hands to help you out here!

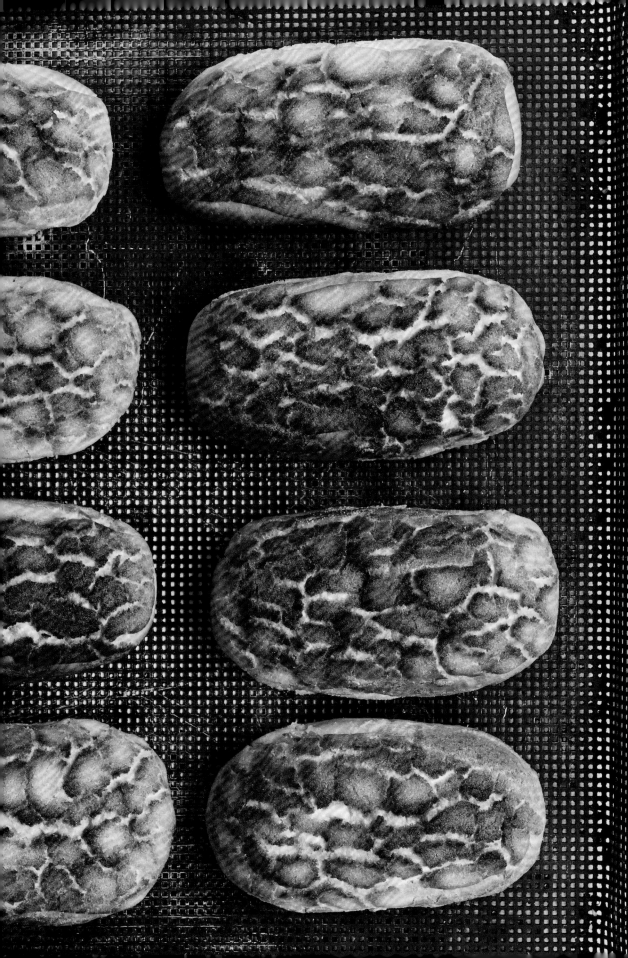

Cheesy Herb and Spinach Buns

MAKES 12 BUNS

⅔ cup (150 ml) lukewarm water (90-100°F/32-38°C)

2¼ tsp instant dry yeast

3⅓ cups (500 g) all-purpose flour

2 Tbsp (25 g) granulated sugar

2 tsp kosher salt

¼ cup (60 g) Philadelphia-style cream cheese

2 Tbsp (30 g) unsalted butter, at room temperature

2 eggs, at room temperature

3 cups (270 g) coarsely grated Cheddar cheese, divided

1 cup (100 g) finely grated Asiago or Parmesan cheese, divided

2 cups (100 g) baby spinach, stems removed

1 cup (20 g) loosely packed fresh herbs (such as basil, chives, green onions, parsley, dill, or chervil), roughly chopped, divided

1 tsp roughly chopped fresh rosemary leaves

1 Tbsp whole milk

We make these on a rotating basis at Crust, and our customers typically ask for them to be used for sandwiches. They're a staff favorite too, so when there are some left over, there's always a raucous round or two of rock-paper-scissors to see who gets to take them home! They are excellent warm out of the oven, with the cream cheese in the dough giving them a bit of richness and tang that goes nicely with the herbs and cheeses. Can I be so cheeky as to say that these are one of my favorite ways to get a dose of daily greens?

1. In a stand mixer, combine the water and yeast, stirring well. Let sit for 10 minutes.

2. Add the flour, sugar, salt, cream cheese, butter, and eggs. Using the dough hook attachment, mix on medium-low speed for about 2 minutes or until the dough comes together. Increase the speed to medium-high and mix for another 6–8 minutes or until the dough looks silky smooth and doesn't stick to the sides of the bowl. You may need to scrape dough off the hook occasionally, or even take the dough out of the bowl and knead it by hand for a few minutes to get it looking silky smooth. Resist adding more flour.

3. Remove the dough from the bowl, lightly brush or spray the bowl with a neutral oil, and return the dough to the bowl. Cover with plastic wrap and set in a warm place (see note on page 179) for 30–45 minutes or until the dough has doubled in size.

4. Line two large sheet pans with parchment paper. Tip the dough onto a lightly floured surface. Using lightly floured fingertips, gently press it into a rectangle. Using a lightly floured rolling pin, roll it into a 9 × 13-inch (23 × 33 cm) rectangle, about ¼ inch (6 mm) thick.

5. Lay the dough with a long side toward you. Leaving a 1-inch (2.5 cm) strip at the top bare, sprinkle 1¾ cups (160 g) of the Cheddar and ¼ cup (25 g) of the Asiago evenly all over the dough, followed by the spinach. Set aside 1 tablespoon of the soft herbs, then sprinkle the rest over the spinach, followed by the rosemary. Moisten the top border with a bit of water, then carefully roll the dough tightly into a log, starting with the side closest to you. (This can be a messy process, but it doesn't have to be perfect.) Cut the roll into twelve equal pieces.

6. Place six buns on each prepared pan, so that you can see the spiral of herbs and cheese on top, leaving as much space between the buns as possible. Cover the buns loosely with plastic wrap and place the pans in your warm proofing spot for 40–60 minutes or until the buns are about one and a half times their original size. You will prepare and bake one pan at a time, so leave the second pan in its warm spot until you are ready for it.

7. Meanwhile, preheat the oven to 350°F (180°C).

8. Brush the tops of the buns on the first pan with milk and sprinkle with half of the remaining Cheddar, Asiago, and herbs.

9. Bake for 12–15 minutes, rotating the pan after 8 minutes to ensure even baking, or until the top and sides of each bun are golden brown. Transfer the buns to a wire rack to cool.

10. Repeat steps 8 and 9 with the second pan of buns.

    These buns are best the day they are made, but will keep in an airtight container at room temperature for up to 2 days, in the fridge for up to 1 week, or in the freezer for up to 1 month.

Crusty Bread Rolls

Poolish

1½ cups (225 g) bread flour (see page 12)

1 cup + 2 Tbsp (280 ml) cold water (60-70°F/ 15-20°C)

¼ tsp instant dry yeast

Dough

4⅓ cups (650 g) bread flour (see page 12)

1½ cups (375 ml) lukewarm water (90-100°F/32-38°C)

2 tsp kosher salt

1 tsp instant dry yeast

4 tsp sesame, poppy, or sunflower seeds (optional)

A poolish is a type of preferment that gives bread a slight sour note and a deep flavor. Using a poolish will also help the bread have a thinner, crispy crust, which is perfect for crusty bread rolls. These rolls are good for sandwiches, alongside a bowl of soup, sliced and eaten with butter and jam, or for that midnight snack once everyone has left the party. They are not light and airy, but have more of a dense, chewy crumb, making them suitable for sopping up gravy or carrying extra slices of ham and cheese. In fact, they're great for anything!

1. **MAKE THE POOLISH:** The day before baking the bread, in a medium mixing bowl, combine the flour, water, and yeast. Using a Danish dough whisk or a fork, blend for about 1 minute or until a very loose dough forms. Cover the bowl loosely with plastic wrap and let ferment at room temperature for 15–24 hours.

2. **MAKE THE DOUGH:** In a stand mixer, combine the poolish, flour, water, salt, and yeast. Using the dough hook attachment, mix on low speed until a rough-looking dough forms, 2–3 minutes.

3. Increase the mixer speed to medium-high and mix until the dough looks smooth, about 6 minutes. The dough should not stick to the bottom of the bowl during this process; instead, it should "clean" the sides of the bowl as it mixes, pulling away from the sides into a cohesive ball. If it seems too sticky, add 1 teaspoon of flour. If it seems too dry and isn't coming together, add 1 teaspoon of water. It is better to err on the sticky side, as you can adjust by adding more flour during kneading. It is harder to add water once the dough comes together. Stop the mixer several times throughout the mixing process to scrape the dough off the dough hook, if needed.

4. Remove the dough from the bowl and lightly spray or brush the bowl with a neutral oil. Return the dough to the bowl, cover the bowl with plastic wrap, and set it in a warm place (see note on page 179) for 1 hour to ferment.

5. Keeping the dough in the bowl, pick up the far edge with both hands and pull it upward, stretching it and gently folding it in half toward you, over top of itself. Rotate the bowl ninety degrees and gently stretch and fold the dough in half over itself again. Cover it again with plastic wrap and let it continue fermenting for another hour, until smooth and at least doubled in size.

continued →

6. Cover the buns with plastic wrap and place the pan in your warm proofing spot for 45–60 minutes or until the buns are about one and a half times their original size and are just touching.

7. Meanwhile, preheat the oven to 350°F (175°C).

8. **MAKE THE CROSS MIX**: In a small mixing bowl, mix the flour, sugar, and cold water until a smooth, slightly runny, pipeable paste forms. To test the consistency, run your finger through it; if it fills in on itself, it's too loose. Adjust with a little extra flour if needed.

9. Transfer the cross mix to a piping bag with a small (3 mm) round tip (or use a small plastic food storage bag and snip the corner to form a 3 mm hole). Starting at the end of one row of buns, pipe the cross mix in a straight, even line across the middle of the buns, all the way to the other end. Repeat for the second and third rows, then pipe across the middle of the buns in the other direction, forming a cross on each bun.

10. Bake for 20–25 minutes or until the tops of the buns are deep golden brown.

11. **MAKE THE GLAZE:** Just before the buns are ready, whisk together the jam and water. In a small pot over medium-low heat, or in the microwave, heat the jam mixture until it is warmed through and has a runnier consistency, easy for brushing. Depending on your jam, it may have a bit of texture from the apricots. If you prefer a smooth glaze, feel free to strain the mixture once it's heated.

12. Transfer the buns to a wire rack and, while still warm, brush the tops with the jam mixture. Let cool slightly before serving.

These buns will keep in an airtight container at room temperature for about 2 days or well wrapped in the fridge for up to 1 week or in the freezer for up to 1 month.

KITCHEN NOTES:

1. Pumpkin spice, also known as pumpkin pie spice or mixed spice, is a mix of warm spices such as cinnamon, nutmeg, ginger, and cloves. If you can't find a premade blend, combine 1 teaspoon ground allspice, 1 teaspoon ground nutmeg, ½ teaspoon ground ginger, ¼ teaspoon ground cloves, and ¼ teaspoon ground white pepper.

2. You might enjoy changing up the standard cross mix a little, as I do sometimes at the shop. After the buns have cooled, brush them with the apricot glaze, then use your favorite frosting to create the cross pattern on top. My favorite is a mixture of 1 cup (130 g) icing sugar, ½ teaspoon pure vanilla extract, and 2-3 teaspoons cream or milk (adding more if needed for a pipeable icing consistency).

PB&J Banana Bread

1 cup (200 g) granulated sugar

½ cup (100 g) dark brown sugar, lightly packed

½ tsp kosher salt

2 eggs, at room temperature

1 cup (300 g) roughly chopped overripe bananas (about 2 large; see note)

½ cup (125 ml) crunchy peanut butter

⅓ cup (75 ml) whole milk

⅓ cup (75 ml) vegetable oil

1 tsp pure vanilla extract

1⅔ cups (250 g) all-purpose flour

2 tsp baking powder

⅓ cup (110 g) raspberry jam

2 Tbsp (25 g) coarse sugar

1 banana, sliced lengthwise on an angle into 3 pieces, for decorating

This is Crust's take on a well-loved classic: the sweetness and depth of jam (perhaps homemade, if you're so inclined), the creaminess of a ripe banana, and the crunchy, savory flavor of peanut butter, all rolled up into a sweet, delicious bread. I always encourage a cup of hot tea or coffee with any sweet afternoon treat, and strive for this type of break on any day that allows it. Hot tip: brush a slice with a little butter and pan-fry for a couple of minutes on each side. Top with a drizzle of maple syrup and eat for breakfast. You're welcome.

1. Preheat the oven to 350°F (180°C). Spray an 8½ × 4½-inch (22 × 11 cm) loaf pan with a neutral oil, then line with two strips of parchment paper, one lengthwise and one widthwise, leaving 1–2 inches (2.5–5 cm) hanging over each of the four edges.

2. In a stand mixer, combine the granulated sugar, brown sugar, salt, eggs, bananas, and peanut butter. Using the paddle attachment, mix on low speed until the bananas are mashed up but retain a little lumpiness, 20–30 seconds. Add the milk, oil, and vanilla and mix on low speed until well combined, 20–30 seconds.

3. Using a fine-mesh sieve, sift the flour and baking powder into the mixer bowl. (You may need to remove the bowl from the stand first.) Gently pulse about ten times or until the flour is incorporated. Using a spatula, scrape down the sides of the bowl, then give it a short burst or two at medium-high speed to ensure any pockets of flour get knocked out. Be careful not to overmix, and increase the speed one setting at a time to ensure batter doesn't fly around the kitchen!

4. Pour half of the batter into the prepared pan and smooth the top with a small spatula.

5. Soften the raspberry jam a little by stirring it with a spoon. Spoon half of it evenly on top of the batter. Pour the remaining batter into the pan and repeat with the remaining jam. Using a butter knife, gently swirl the jam through the batter a few times to evenly distribute a swirly pattern through the whole loaf. Sprinkle the top with the coarse sugar.

6. Bake for 15 minutes. Carefully place the banana slices, cut side up, diagonally on top of the loaf. (Try not to move the loaf around too much while doing this, or it will deflate.) Bake for another 60–70 minutes or until the loaf is deep golden brown and a skewer inserted in the center comes out clean. Let cool in the pan for 15 minutes, then gently lift the loaf using the overhanging parchment paper and transfer to a wire rack to cool completely.

This banana bread should be eaten at room temperature and will keep for about a week, covered, in the fridge. I find it easiest to slice and individually

wrap each piece with plastic wrap before refrigerating so that anyone in the household can grab a piece and go! You can also pack the wrapped slices in a large freezer bag and freeze for up to 2 months.

KITCHEN NOTES:

1. It's easy to undercook this loaf, so make sure the center has fully risen and the skewer comes out clean. If you are worried that the loaf is getting dark too early, cover it loosely with parchment paper or foil and continue baking until done.

Buttery Brioche

2⅔ cups (400 g) bread flour (see page 12), divided

2¼ tsp instant dry yeast

⅓ cup + 1 Tbsp (90 ml) lukewarm whole milk (90-100°F/32-38°C)

5 eggs, at room temperature, divided

2 Tbsp (25 g) granulated sugar

1½ tsp kosher salt

1 cup (225 g) unsalted butter, at room temperature, cut into ½-inch (1.2 cm) cubes

Brioche, in many variations, is a staple at Crust. It is packed with creamy butter, so what's not to love? It toasts up beautifully, it can be sweet or savory, and it is a relatively easy and forgiving dough to make. At Crust, we make sandwiches with brioche bread and buns, varying the fillings by season and imagination. Brioche is slightly on the sweet side and pairs beautifully with tangy mustard, salty ham, and sliced tomatoes.

1. In a stand mixer bowl, whisk together ⅔ cup (100 g) of the flour and the yeast and milk. Cover the bowl with plastic wrap and ferment in a warm place (see note on page 179) for about 45 minutes or until doubled in size.

2. Place the bowl in the stand mixer and add four of the eggs, the remaining flour, and the sugar and salt. Using the paddle attachment, mix on medium-low speed for about 1 minute or until just combined. Increase the speed to medium-high and mix for 2–3 minutes or until the dough is smooth and silky. You may need to stop the mixer and scrape down the paddle and the sides of the bowl several times. Let rest for about 5 minutes.

3. Set the mixer to medium speed and add the butter, one cube at a time, making sure each piece is incorporated before adding the next. Scrape down the bowl and the paddle regularly between additions. If you find the paddle is having trouble moving through the dough, switch to the dough hook. The dough will look very sticky, and that's what you want. Mix on medium-high speed for another 6–8 minutes or until the dough looks smooth and feels soft and silky.

4. Remove the dough from the bowl and lightly spray or brush the bowl with a neutral oil. Return the dough to the bowl, cover the bowl with plastic wrap, and immediately place it in the fridge. Refrigerate for at least 4 hours or preferably overnight. The dough must be very cold when you're shaping it, or it will be sticky and difficult to handle.

5. Remove the dough from the bowl and cut it in half. Cut each half into four equal pieces. Working with one piece at a time, use your thumbs and the heels of both hands to pull the dough taut from the top as you wobble and tuck it underneath itself to the bottom, forming a ball with a top that is tight and smooth.

6. Spray or brush two 8½ × 4½ (22 × 11 cm) loaf pans with a neutral oil. Place four of the balls, smooth side up, in each pan. Cover the pans with plastic wrap and place them in your warm proofing spot for 1–2 hours or until the loaves have almost doubled in size.

7. Meanwhile, preheat the oven to 350°F (180°C).

8. In a small bowl, whisk the remaining egg with 1 tablespoon of water. Brush the tops of the loaves with the egg wash.

9. Bake for 40–50 minutes or until the loaves are deep golden brown, the bottoms sound hollow when tapped, and the internal temperature reaches 190°F (88°C). Remove the loaves from the pans and let cool on a wire rack for at least 1 hour before serving.

   This bread will keep in an airtight container at room temperature for up to 3 days or in the freezer for up to 1 month. I suggest slicing it before you freeze it so that you can take out one slice at a time and pop it in the toaster.

KITCHEN NOTE:

1. Unbaked brioche dough freezes quite well, wrapped tightly, for about 2 weeks. Thaw it in the fridge overnight, then shape, proof, and bake as per steps 5-9.

Cinnamon Brioche Scrolls

Dough

2⅔ cups (400 g) bread
flour (see page 12),
divided

2¼ tsp instant dry yeast

⅓ cup + 1 Tbsp (90 ml)
lukewarm whole milk
(90-100°F/32-38°C)

4 eggs, at room temperature

2 Tbsp (25 g) granulated
sugar

1½ tsp kosher salt

1 cup (225 g) unsalted
butter, at room
temperature, cut into
½-inch (1.2 cm) cubes

Filling

1 cup (200 g) dark brown
sugar, lightly packed

½ cup (115 g) unsalted
butter, at room temperature

2 Tbsp (18 g) ground
cinnamon

2 tsp pure vanilla extract

¼ tsp kosher salt

1 recipe Lemon Cream
Cheese Frosting (page 243;
see note)

Absolute decadence, these scrolls are the elevated version of the typical cinnamon bun. If you are so inclined, they make a wonderful Christmas morning breakfast, fresh-baked as an indulgent treat post–gift giving or to greet guests as they arrive for hot cocoa. (Warning—the scent of them baking may have the neighborhood at your door.) While I love them just the way they are, my wife puts in chocolate chips when she makes them. If that appeals, fill your boots!

———

1. **MAKE THE DOUGH:** In a stand mixer bowl, whisk together ⅔ cup (100 g) of the flour and the yeast and milk. Cover the bowl with plastic wrap and ferment in a warm place (see note on page 179) for about 45 minutes or until doubled in size.

2. Place the bowl in the stand mixer and add the eggs, the remaining flour, and the sugar and salt. Using the paddle attachment, mix on medium-low speed for about 1 minute or until combined. Increase the speed to medium-high and mix for 2–3 minutes. You may need to stop the mixer and scrape down the paddle and the sides of the bowl several times. Let rest for about 5 minutes.

3. Set the mixer to medium speed and add the butter, one cube at a time, making sure each piece is incorporated before adding the next. Scrape down the bowl and the paddle regularly between additions. If you find the paddle is having trouble moving through the dough, switch to the dough hook. The dough will look very sticky, and that's what you want. Mix on medium-high speed for another 6–8 minutes or until the dough looks smooth and feels soft and silky.

4. Remove the dough from the bowl and lightly spray or brush the bowl with a neutral oil. Return the dough to the bowl, cover the bowl with plastic wrap, and immediately place it in the fridge. Refrigerate for at least 4 hours or preferably overnight. The dough must be very cold when you're shaping it, or it will be sticky and difficult to handle.

5. Spray or brush an 8 × 12-inch (20 × 30 cm) baking pan with a neutral oil and line the bottom with parchment paper.

6. **MAKE THE FILLING:** In a medium bowl, mix together the brown sugar, butter, cinnamon, vanilla, and salt until soft and well combined.

7. **TO ASSEMBLE:** Tip the dough onto a lightly floured surface and cut it in half. Using lightly floured fingertips, press the first half into a rectangle. Using a lightly floured rolling pin, roll it into a 9 × 13-inch (23 × 33 cm) rectangle, about ¼ inch (6 mm) thick. Repeat with the other half.

continued →

7. In a medium bowl, mix ¾ cup (75 g) of the Parmesan and the butter, chives, flaky salt, and pepper. The mixture should be very soft and spreadable. (I find it easiest to do this if the butter is really soft, so warm it a bit if needed, but do not melt it.) Stir in the leeks until well combined.

8. **TO ASSEMBLE:** Tip the dough onto a lightly floured surface and cut it in half. Using lightly floured fingertips, press the first half into a rectangle. Using a lightly floured rolling pin, roll it into a 9 × 13-inch (23 × 33 cm) rectangle, about ¼ inch (6 mm) thick. Repeat with the other half.

9. Lay one rectangle with a long side toward you. Spread half of the filling evenly over the dough, leaving a 1-inch (2.5 cm) strip at the top bare. Roll up the dough, starting with the side closest to you and finishing with the seam on the bottom. Repeat with the second rectangle.

10. Using a knife or unflavored dental floss, cut each roll into six even scrolls. Place the scrolls, cut side down, in the prepared pan. Cover the pan loosely with plastic wrap and place it in your warm proofing spot for 40–60 minutes or until the scrolls are almost doubled in size.

11. Meanwhile, preheat the oven to 350°F (180°C).

12. Sprinkle each scroll with the remaining Parmesan. Finish with a little extra cracked black pepper and flaky sea salt, if you like.

13. Bake for 15–20 minutes or until the tops of the scrolls are golden brown. If they are browning too much, tent loosely with foil after 12 minutes. Serve immediately. (I love for my guests to pull the scrolls apart themselves, right at the table!)

These scrolls will keep in an airtight container at room temperature for up to 2 days or in the freezer for up to 2 weeks.

KITCHEN NOTES:

1. Use only the white and light green parts of the leek. If you can't get your hands on a leek, you can use a white onion.

2. Asiago cheese is a fair substitute for fresh Parmesan, and is a little less expensive.

Brioche Doughnuts

with Lemon Curd

Doughnuts

2⅔ cups (400 g) bread
flour (see page 12),
divided

2¼ tsp instant dry yeast

⅓ cup + 1 Tbsp (90 ml)
lukewarm whole milk
(90-100°F/32-38°C)

4 eggs, at room temperature

2 Tbsp (25 g) granulated
sugar

1 tsp finely grated lemon
zest

1 tsp kosher salt

½ cup (115 g) unsalted
butter, at room
temperature, cut into
½-inch (1.2 cm) cubes

5 cups (1.25 L) neutral
oil, such as canola

1 recipe Lemon Curd
(page 251), cold (see note)

Cinnamon Sugar

1 cup (200 g) granulated
sugar

1 Tbsp ground cinnamon

Lemon curd doughnuts! The best of both worlds. I cannot even begin to tell you how good these are. When I was a kid, we occasionally made doughnuts as a family on the weekend. The extra hands were welcomed, as there are several steps and stages, and having someone to hold the cooked doughnut while you pipe in the curd is especially helpful. This recipe makes a lot—if you are going to spend the time to make them, there might as well be one for everyone!

1. **MAKE THE DOUGHNUTS:** In a stand mixer bowl, whisk together ⅔ cup (100 g) of the flour and the yeast and milk. Cover the bowl with plastic wrap and ferment in a warm place (see note on page 179) for about 45 minutes or until doubled in size.

2. Place the bowl in the stand mixer and add the eggs, the remaining flour, and the sugar, lemon zest, and salt. Using the paddle attachment, mix on medium-low speed for about 1 minute or until combined. Increase the speed to medium-high and mix for 2–3 minutes. You may need to stop the mixer and scrape down the paddle and the sides of the bowl several times. Let rest for about 5 minutes.

3. Set the mixer to medium speed and add the butter, one cube at a time, making sure each piece is incorporated before adding the next. Scrape down the bowl and the paddle regularly between additions. If you find the paddle is having trouble moving through the dough, switch to the dough hook. The dough will look very sticky, and that's what you want. Mix on medium-high speed for another 6–8 minutes or until the dough looks smooth and feels soft and silky.

4. Remove the dough from the bowl and lightly spray or brush the bowl with a neutral oil. Return the dough to the bowl, cover the bowl with plastic wrap, and immediately place it in the fridge. Refrigerate for at least 4 hours or preferably overnight. The dough must be very cold when you're shaping it, or it will be sticky and difficult to handle.

5. Line two large sheet pans with parchment paper. Tip the dough onto a lightly floured surface. Using a lightly floured rolling pin, roll the dough into a 5 × 12-inch (13 × 30 cm) rectangle, ¾–1 inch (2–2.5 cm) thick. Using a pastry scraper or dull knife, cut the dough in half lengthwise to form two long strips. Cut each strip into eight equal pieces .

6. Working with one piece at a time, use your thumbs and the heels of both hands to pull the dough taut from the top as you wobble and tuck it underneath itself to the bottom, forming a ball with a top that is tight and smooth. Place the ball, smooth side up, on a prepared pan. Continue forming balls, making two rows of four on each pan and leaving as much space as possible in between.

continued →

7. Cover the doughnuts loosely with lightly greased plastic wrap and place the pans in your warm proofing spot for 2–3 hours or until the doughnuts have doubled in size. They will be delicate at this stage, so be very gentle with them.

8. When the doughnuts are almost ready, heat the oil to 350°F (180°C) in a large, heavy-bottomed pot (or better yet a deep fryer), checking regularly with a thermometer. Line a large rimmed sheet pan with paper towels or an unbleached paper bag and set it nearby.

9. **MAKE THE CINNAMON SUGAR:** In a large shallow bowl, stir together the sugar and cinnamon until well combined.

10. Using tongs or a slotted spoon, carefully place two or three doughnuts in the hot oil (see note). Be very gentle with them so as not to deflate them (and, of course, be very careful with the hot oil). Monitor the temperature of the oil and adjust the heat accordingly. After 45–60 seconds, when the doughnuts are light golden brown, gently turn them over and fry for another 45–60 seconds. Turn and cook them twice more, so the doughnuts have had 3–4 minutes total in the hot oil. They should be a beautiful golden brown, with a pale ring around the middle. Using a slotted spoon, transfer them to the lined rimmed pan and let sit for about 1 minute, then move on quickly to the next step. You want the excess oil to drain, but for the doughnut to still be warm so that the sugar sticks.

11. Using two forks or your hands, add each doughnut to the cinnamon sugar and toss very gently, then return to the pan. They are very delicate, so be careful with them!

12. Repeat steps 10 and 11 with the remaining doughnuts, in batches of two or three at a time. Let cool completely on the pan before stuffing them.

13. Fill a piping bag (or a plastic food storage bag) with the lemon curd and snip a ½-inch (1.2 cm) corner off the end (or one corner).

14. Using a small knife, make an incision about 1 inch (2.5 cm) wide and 2 inches (5 cm) deep in each doughnut, along the pale equator. (This is where it is helpful to have more than one person! If you are working solo, set each doughnut upright in one cup of a muffin tin to help stabilize it as you stuff it.) Pipe about 1 tablespoon of curd into each doughnut until a little bit peeks out of the hole. Serve immediately.

These doughnuts are unquestionably best eaten the day they are made, but they do keep in an airtight container at room temperature for 1 more day. Before stuffing, they can be well wrapped and frozen for up to 1 month.

KITCHEN NOTES:

1. You can replace the lemon curd with other curds, chocolate mousse, cream, or jams if you like.

2. It is important to maintain a consistent temperature while you are cooking the doughnuts, so don't overcrowd the pot or deep fryer. How many doughnuts you can add at once will depend on the size of your pot. They will grow as they fry, so be mindful of that if you have a smaller pot.

Old-School Bagels

<u>Dough</u>

5 cups (750 g) bread flour
(see page 12)

2 Tbsp (25 g) granulated
sugar

4 tsp (20 g) kosher salt

2¼ tsp instant dry yeast

3 Tbsp (45 ml) vegetable oil

1¾ cups (425 ml) lukewarm
water (90-100°F/32-38°C)

<u>For the Poaching Water</u>

12 cups (3 L) water

2 Tbsp (25 g) light brown
sugar, lightly packed

1 Tbsp kosher salt

1 Tbsp baking soda

<u>Toppings</u>

1 egg white, whisked with
2 tsp cold water

2 Tbsp everything bagel
mix, sesame seeds, or
poppy seeds, or 2 tsp
flaky sea salt

Scan for
bagel-shaping
tips

Chewy, flavorful homemade bagels are a far cry from the mass-produced ones you buy at the grocery store, and practicing the technique of rolling, boiling, and baking is really worth it. (I love making them for this interesting process alone!) Not long ago, I made a batch for my son and his friends to eat after an epic hockey game. Following the cacophony of a bunch of teenage boys in my house, I wandered into the kitchen to offer them some, only to find that they had already demolished each and every one, still a bit warm, poppy and sesame seeds everywhere, a satisfied grin on every face.

1. **MAKE THE DOUGH:** In a stand mixer, combine the flour, granulated sugar, salt, yeast, and oil. Pour in the water. Using the dough hook attachment, mix on medium-low speed for about 30 seconds or until the dough just comes together. Increase the speed to medium-high and mix for 4–5 minutes or until the dough looks silky smooth and doesn't stick to the sides of the bowl. You may need to scrape off the dough hook occasionally during the mixing process.

2. Remove the dough from the bowl and lightly brush or spray the bowl with neutral oil. Return the dough to the bowl, cover the bowl with plastic wrap, and place it in a warm place (see note on page 179) for 30–45 minutes or until the dough has doubled in size.

3. Line three large sheet pans with parchment paper. Lightly brush or spray the parchment with a neutral oil.

4. Tip the dough onto a lightly floured surface. Using lightly floured hands, press it firmly into a 14 × 8-inch (35 × 20 cm) rectangle, about ½ inch (1.2 cm) thick. Using a pastry scraper or dull knife, cut it into twelve equal pieces.

5. Wipe all the flour off the counter, then use a damp cloth to wipe the counter so it's left slightly damp.

6. Working with one piece of dough at a time, firmly flatten it into a 3 × 6-inch (7.5 × 15 cm) rectangle. Lay it with a long side toward you, then carefully fold the top third down. Using the heel of your hand, lightly hammer the folded dough to remove any air bubbles. Fold it once more and gently hammer to form a 1-inch (2.5 cm) wide cylinder, about 6 inches (15 cm) long. Roll the dough back and forth with both hands until it is even and about 9–10 inches (23–25 cm) long. Using the heel of your hand, flatten out 2 inches (5 cm) on either end of the cylinder, then join the two ends together, squeezing and pinching to secure the ends in place. (Scan the QR code for a how-to video.)

continued →

7. You now have a bagel-shaped piece of dough. Holding it with one hand as though you are about to roll it along the counter like a tire, place two fingers from your other hand through the hole and roll forward and backward while you also slowly roll the bagel along the counter. The finished bagel should be about 4 inches (10 cm) in diameter, with a 2-inch (5 cm) hole in the center. (Rolling bagels is an art and an acquired skill! Don't worry if you don't get it perfect the first time.) Place the bagel on a prepared pan.

8. Repeat steps 6 and 7 to make twelve bagels, placing four on each pan. Cover the bagels loosely with plastic wrap and place the pans in your warm proofing spot for 30–50 minutes or until the bagels are one and a half times their original size. (When you move on to poaching the bagels, do not discard the oiled parchment on the pans.)

9. **PREPARE THE POACHING WATER:** In a large, wide pot, combine the water, brown sugar, salt, and baking soda. Stir well and bring to a boil over high heat.

10. Preheat the oven to 500°F (260°C).

11. Lower the heat to a simmer and carefully place three bagels in the poaching water. Cook for 30 seconds, then use tongs or a slotted spoon to carefully flip them over and cook for another 30 seconds. Transfer the bagels to a wire rack set over a clean kitchen towel and let drain. Repeat with the remaining bagels, in batches of three at a time.

12. Return the poached bagels to the lined pans. Brush them with the egg wash, then sprinkle the tops generously with your desired topping.

13. Place one or two pans in the oven (depending on space) and lower the temperature to 440°F (227°C). Bake for 15–20 minutes, rotating the pans after 8 minutes, until the bagels are beautifully golden brown. Transfer the bagels to a wire rack to cool for at least 30 minutes before eating or slicing.

These bagels will keep in an airtight container at room temperature for up to 3 days, in the fridge for up to 1 week, or in the freezer for up to 1 month.

KITCHEN NOTES:

1. I like to prepare the bagels through step 8, then place them in the fridge overnight and cook them in the morning. That way, they proof slowly and develop a nicer flavor, and I can have fresh bagels for breakfast!

2. Leftover bagels that are on the verge of becoming stale make excellent croutons. Slice them into thin rounds, toss with garlic and olive oil, and pop them into a 350°F (180°C) oven for 15 minutes or so. Sprinkle them over salads or use them to scoop up onion dip.

Baking Staples

"I'm living on things that excite me,
be they pastry or lobster or love."

JIMMY BUFFETT

PASTRY

Everyone needs a good pie crust or two (or three). Even after all these years, it still amazes me that with just a few tweaks to the ingredients, techniques, and methods, pastry can be quite different from one recipe to the next. Whether it's the addition of shortening or sugar, the temperature of the water, or which machine is used to mix the ingredients, each pastry has its place. In the following pages, we offer different pastries for different needs, along with a variety of ways to mix the dough.

Basic Pastry

MAKES ENOUGH FOR TWO
9-INCH (23 CM) PIE CRUSTS

2½ cups (375 g) all-purpose flour

2 Tbsp (25 g) granulated sugar

1 tsp kosher salt

¾ cup (175 g) cold unsalted butter, cut into ½-inch (1.2 cm) cubes

½ cup (100 g) cold vegetable shortening, cut into ½-inch (1.2 cm) cubes

½ cup (125 ml) ice water

2 tsp white vinegar

1. In a food processor fitted with the S blade (see note), pulse together the flour, sugar, and salt. Add the butter and shortening and pulse until the mixture forms small pieces, about the size of peas. The dough should be a little rough, with butter speckled throughout. Add the ice water, 1 tablespoon at a time, and pulse until the dough just comes together. It should be moist, but not wet.

2. Tip the dough onto a lightly floured surface and gather it into two equal balls, without handling or working it too much. Using lightly floured fingertips, flatten the balls into 5-inch (13 cm) disks, about ¾ inch (2 cm) thick. Wrap tightly in plastic wrap and refrigerate for at least 1 hour before using.

This pastry will keep, well wrapped, in the fridge for up to 3 days or in the freezer for up to 1 month. Thaw frozen pastry in the fridge for 1 day before using.

KITCHEN NOTE:

1. If you don't have a food processor, you can combine the flour, sugar, and salt in a large mixing bowl and use a pastry cutter or a fork to cut in the butter and shortening until you get pea-sized chunks. Blend the ice water into the dough using a fork until the dough just comes together.

Sweet Pastry

1 cup (150 g) all-purpose flour

⅔ cup (100 g) cake or pastry flour (see note)

½ cup (115 g) unsalted butter, at room temperature

½ cup (100 g) granulated sugar

¼ tsp kosher salt

1 egg, at room temperature

1 tsp pure vanilla extract

1. Using a fine-mesh sieve, sift the all-purpose flour and cake flour into a bowl.

2. In a stand mixer, combine the butter, sugar, and salt. Using the paddle attachment, beat on high speed until well blended, pale, and creamy, about 3 minutes. Add the egg and vanilla and beat for another minute, until combined. Scrape down the sides of the bowl to ensure all the ingredients are well incorporated. Add the flour mixture and mix on low speed just until the flour is just mixed in. Do not overmix.

3. Divide the mixture in half and squish each half with the heel of your palm to make a ½-inch (1.2 cm) thick disk. Wrap tightly in plastic wrap and refrigerate for at least 1 hour, or preferably overnight, before using.

This pastry will keep, well wrapped, in the fridge for up to 3 days or in the freezer for up to 1 month. Thaw frozen pastry in the fridge for 1 day before using.

KITCHEN NOTE:

1. Although pastry flour is preferred for its low gluten content, don't worry if you don't have it. All-purpose flour will be fine with the same measurements (see page 12).

Chocolate Pastry

½ cup (115 g) unsalted butter, at room temperature

½ cup (100 g) granulated sugar

¼ tsp kosher salt

1 egg, at room temperature

1 tsp pure vanilla extract

⅔ cup (100 g) all-purpose flour

½ cup + 2 Tbsp (90 g) cake or pastry flour

⅓ cup (35 g) cocoa powder

1. In a stand mixer, combine the butter, sugar, and salt. Using the paddle attachment, beat on medium-high speed until well blended, pale, and creamy, about 90 seconds. Add the egg and vanilla and mix for another 30 seconds. Scrape down the sides of the bowl to ensure all the ingredients are well incorporated.

2. Using a fine-mesh sieve, sift the all-purpose flour, cake flour, and cocoa into the mixer bowl. Mix on low speed for about 30 seconds or until the flours and cocoa are just mixed in. Do not overmix.

3. Squish the dough into a 7-inch (18 cm) disk, about 1 inch (2.5 cm) thick. Wrap tightly in plastic wrap and refrigerate for at least 1 hour, or preferably overnight, before using.

This pastry will keep, well wrapped, in the fridge for up to 3 days or in the freezer for up to 1 month. Thaw frozen pastry in the fridge for 1 day before using.

Sour Cream Pastry

2⅔ cups (400 g) all-purpose flour

1 Tbsp granulated sugar

½ tsp kosher salt

1 cup (225 g) cold unsalted butter, cut into ½-inch (1.2 cm) cubes

1 cup (250 ml) full-fat (14%) sour cream

1 Tbsp white vinegar

2 tsp ice water

1. In a large mixing bowl, whisk together the flour, sugar, and salt. Add the butter. Using a pastry cutter, a fork, or your fingers, cut or squeeze the butter into the flour until the mixture resembles coarse meal with small chunks of flattened butter throughout. Using a fork, stir in the sour cream and vinegar. Mix gently for about 15 seconds or until the dough just starts to come together.

2. Tip the dough onto a clean counter and add the ice water. Using your palm or a pastry scraper, smear the dough across the countertop several times until it just comes together. It should be moist, but not wet, and a little rough, with pea-sized pieces of flattened butter disks throughout.

3. Gently pat the dough together to form an 8-inch (20 cm) square, about 1 inch (2.5 cm) thick. The dough should look a bit lumpy and slightly undermixed.

4. Cut the dough in half and place one half on the other. Using lightly floured fingertips, gently press the dough into an 8-inch (20 cm) square, about 1 inch (2.5 cm) thick.

5. Cut the dough in half again and place one half on top of the other. This time, use a floured rolling pin to gently roll it into an 8-inch (20 cm) square, about 1 inch (2.5 cm) thick. Wrap tightly in plastic wrap and refrigerate for at least 1 hour before using.

This pastry will keep, well wrapped, in the fridge for up to 3 days or in the freezer for up to 1 month. Thaw frozen pastry in the fridge for 1 day before using.

Savory Pastry

2⅔ cups (400 g) all-purpose flour

¾ cup (175 g) cold unsalted butter, cut into ¼-inch (6 mm) cubes

1 tsp kosher salt

½ cup (125 ml) ice water

1 Tbsp white vinegar

1 egg yolk, cold

1. In a stand mixer, combine the flour, butter, and salt. Using the paddle attachment, beat on low speed until well mixed, 2–3 minutes. The butter will look like pea-sized flattened disks. Don't mix past this point, or your pastry won't be flaky.

2. Tip the mixture onto a clean counter. Make a well in the middle of the flour and add the ice water, vinegar, and egg yolk. Using a plastic bench scraper or large palette knife, cut the flour into the liquid, bit by bit. At this point, it will look like a big shaggy mess, and that's perfectly fine. Using your palm or the bench scraper, gently smear the dough together a little. It will still look a bit messy and not quite mixed together properly.

3. Transfer the dough to the middle of a clean tea towel, in as neat a pile as possible. Gather the corners of the towel and wrap up the bundle firmly to form a round ball inside. Press down firmly on the towel, then unwrap the dough. It should now be a cohesive dough, without being overmixed.

4. Wrap the dough tightly in plastic wrap and press it into a 9-inch (23 cm) disk, about 1 inch (2.5 cm) thick. Refrigerate for at least 1 hour before using. Let warm to room temperature before rolling, and use as little flour as possible for dusting.

   This pastry will keep, well wrapped, in the fridge for up to 3 days or in the freezer for up to 1 month. Thaw frozen pastry in the fridge for 1 day before using.

KITCHEN NOTE:

1. When using this pastry in a recipe, I have found that you can gather the scraps once, as long as you very carefully combine them without overworking. Let rest in the fridge for 30-60 minutes before rerolling.

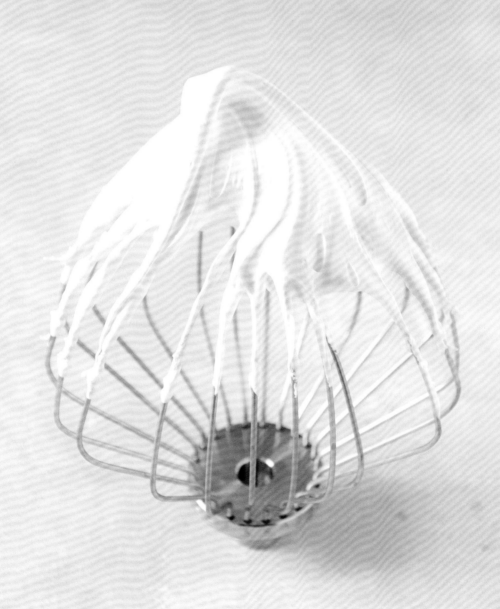

Swiss Meringue

½ cup (125 ml) egg whites (about 4)

1 cup (200 g) granulated sugar

⅛ tsp kosher salt

½ tsp pure vanilla extract

If you've never tried Swiss meringue, I'm so glad you are here! This is unlike any meringue you've had, absolutely delicious on its own, torched for lemon meringue pie or cupcakes, baked into a pavlova, or mixed further to make buttercream.

1. Bring a medium pot with about 1 inch (2.5 cm) of water to a boil, then lower the heat to a simmer.

2. In a stainless steel bowl just big enough to fit snugly on top of the pot without touching the water, whisk together the egg whites and sugar until combined. Place the bowl over the simmering pot and stir slowly but continuously. (If you stop stirring, you will end up with sweet, scrambled eggs!) Heat until the mixture is quite warm, almost hot to the touch, and the sugar has almost dissolved, about 5 minutes. If you'd like to get nerdy, the temperature of the mixture should be between 150°F and 160°F (66°C and 71°C).

3. Carefully remove the bowl from the pot and dry the bottom thoroughly with a towel so that it doesn't drip water when you transfer the mixture.

4. Transfer the egg white mixture to a very clean and dry stand mixer bowl. Add the salt and vanilla and, using the whisk attachment, whisk on high speed for 5–8 minutes or until the sides of the bowl feel like they have cooled to room temperature and the mixture is light and fluffy with stiff peaks that hold their shape. If you rub a wee bit of the meringue between your fingers, it should feel smooth and not gritty, as all the sugar should have dissolved.

5. Use immediately. Meringue will not be usable for more than a few minutes after you turn off the mixer.

KITCHEN NOTES:

1. Make sure your equipment is really clean when making meringue. Any greasy residue on your bowl or whisk will affect the egg white mixture's ability to whip up and hold its shape.

2. Make the meringue as close as possible to when you are going to use it. It will start to collapse fairly quickly and will lose its sheen and gloss. You can hold it for up to 10 minutes by turning the mixer to the lowest speed and letting it run slowly.

3. If you have leftover meringue, pipe out little shapes or mini pavlovas and bake them at 200°F (100°C) for 1-2 hours, depending on their size, until dry and crisp.

Lemon Cream Cheese Frosting

1 cup (250 g) Philadelphia-style cream cheese, at room temperature

½ cup (115 g) unsalted butter, at room temperature

1 cup (130 g) icing sugar, sifted

1 tsp finely grated lemon zest

2 Tbsp (30 ml) fresh lemon juice (see note)

½ tsp pure vanilla extract

I am particular about my icings and frostings. Those that are made with just butter, sugar, and a little flavoring seem cloying and overly sweet to me. I prefer to add a little more depth and creaminess, and the Philadelphia-style cream cheese in this recipe also provides a little zing and some structure, making this frosting much more appropriate for our Signature Carrot Cake (page 131) and Cinnamon Brioche Scrolls (page 221).

1. In a stand mixer, combine the cream cheese and butter. Using the paddle attachment, mix on low speed until combined, then mix on high speed for about 1 minute or until pale and fluffy.

2. Add the sugar and mix on medium-high speed for 1 minute. Add the lemon zest, lemon juice, and vanilla and mix well to combine. Scrape down the bowl to ensure all the ingredients are fully incorporated, then mix for 30 seconds on medium-high speed until completely smooth.

This frosting will keep in an airtight container in the fridge for up to 1 week or in the freezer for up to 1 month. To use, bring it to room temperature, then beat it with the paddle attachment in a stand mixer until smooth and creamy, about 3 minutes.

KITCHEN NOTES:

1. Make sure the butter and cream cheese are at room temperature, or you will get lumps in your frosting.

2. Only use fresh lemon juice, never bottled. It makes all the difference!

3. If the frosting is too thin, cool it in the refrigerator for a few minutes until it thickens up.

4. If you prefer the icing to be a little runnier and easier to drizzle for the Cinnamon Brioche Scrolls, stir in 1-2 teaspoons of whole milk until you achieve the desired consistency.

Dark Chocolate Ganache

MAKES ABOUT 3 CUPS (750 ML)

13 oz (375 g) semisweet
dark chocolate (around
60% cocoa solids), at
room temperature

1½ cups (375 ml) whipping
cream

Chocolate ganache is simple to make, yet its rich decadence makes it seem much more complicated. It works nicely as cake icing or as a spread over a graham base or sweet square. And dare I say a spot of it is warranted on a piece of peanut butter toast? Although chocolate ganache is lovely on its own, whipping takes it to the next level, and is necessary for my Tom Tams (page 161)!

1. Roughly chop the chocolate into ½-inch (1.2 cm) pieces. Place it in a medium heatproof bowl, such as glass or glazed ceramic.

2. In a medium pot, bring the whipping cream to a rolling boil over high heat, about 4 minutes. Keep a close eye on it when it starts to get hot, as it will boil over quickly!

3. Immediately pour the boiling cream over the chocolate. Leave the two ingredients alone for 1–2 minutes to let the chocolate melt a little, so it will combine more quickly and thoroughly with the cream when you stir it.

4. Using a whisk, gently stir until well combined, about 3 minutes. (If you stir too hard or fast, you will get lots of air bubbles, which tend to remain when you use the ganache in a tart or as a glaze, and that can look a bit funny.) When there are no signs of unmelted chocolate left, your ganache is ready to use.

This ganache, once cooled completely, can be stored in a sterile container in the fridge for up to 1 week. When cooling it, place a lid on top but leave it ajar for the first 1–2 hours to avoid condensation. Otherwise, you'll get drops of moisture on top of the ganache that will change its consistency and look, and will make it spoil quickly.

For Whipped Chocolate Ganache

1. Start with ganache that is freshly made, or reheat it (see note) until it is melted and quite warm to the touch, about 140°F (60°C). The temperature is important: if it is too cool, the ganache will split and won't whip.

2. Pour the ganache into a stand mixer bowl and, using the whisk attachment, whip on high speed for 5–8 minutes or until the bottom of the bowl feels like it has cooled to room temperature and the ganache has whipped up, looks a little paler, and has stiffened to the thickness of whipped cream.

KITCHEN NOTES:

1. Dark chocolate ganache is made with a 1:1 ratio of dark chocolate metric weight to whipping cream metric volume, so you can easily make a bigger or smaller batch! For example, to make 2 cups (500 ml) of ganache, use 8 oz (250 g) dark chocolate and 1 cup (250 ml) whipping cream.

2. I love adding a touch of finely grated orange zest to my ganache, or even some ground pink peppercorns or a little cayenne pepper and salt. One to two teaspoons of ground coriander is a lovely, fragrant addition, as is a scant ⅛ teaspoon of rosewater. Add your flavorings a little at a time in step 4, and taste as you go.

3. If you need to soften the ganache after it's been refrigerated, bring a medium pot with about 1 inch (2.5 cm) of water to a boil, then lower the heat to a simmer. Top with a stainless steel bowl that is just big enough to fit snugly on top of the pot without touching the water. Scoop the ganache into the bowl and stir gently with a spatula until it is silky smooth and about 140°F (60°C). Alternatively, you can soften the ganache in a bowl in the microwave for 20 seconds at a time, stirring after each interval, for about 1 minute, until silky smooth and about 140°F (60°C). With either method, be careful not to overheat it, or the chocolate will seize and won't be usable.

Salted Almond Crumble

½ cup (60 g) almond flour, lightly packed

⅓ cup (50 g) all-purpose flour

¼ cup (50 g) granulated sugar

½ tsp kosher salt

3 Tbsp (45 g) cold unsalted butter, cut into ⅛-inch (3 mm) cubes

1 tsp pure vanilla extract

½ cup (50 g) flaked blanched almonds

This crumble is used on the Toffee Poached Apple Pie (page 48) and the Toffee Poached Apple Muffins (page 61), but you can use it on any fruit crumble or bake it on its own (see note) and shake it over ice cream or gelato. Its salty sweetness works well with anything that calls for a crumble, and the almonds give it a little extra crunch.

1. Line a large rimmed sheet pan with parchment paper.

2. In a stand mixer, combine the almond flour, all-purpose flour, sugar, salt, butter, and vanilla. Using the paddle attachment, beat on low speed for 1–2 minutes or until the mixture is well blended and appears crumbly, with crumbs the size of small peas. You don't want to create a dough by overmixing it, so stop the mixer as soon as the crumbly texture is achieved.

3. Remove the bowl from the mixer and gently stir in the almonds.

4. Spread the mixture out on the prepared pan and refrigerate for at least 30 minutes. Crumble over your dessert before baking as directed in the dessert recipe.

   To freeze, place the pan in the freezer for 1–2 hours to set, then transfer the crumble to a large freezer bag and store in the freezer for up to 3 months.

KITCHEN NOTES:

1. If you are not using the crumble the same day you make it, it is best to freeze it. It's very important that it's cold when you use it, so it keeps its shape and doesn't melt into the baked good you are topping.

2. To bake the crumble on its own, spread it on a parchment-lined large rimmed sheet pan and bake in a 350°F (180°C) oven for 20 minutes or until golden brown, stirring occasionally.

Toffee Poached Apples

MAKES ABOUT 5 CUPS (1.25 KG)

2 cups (500 ml)
unsweetened, pure, clear
apple juice

1 cup (200 g) granulated
sugar

¼ cup (60 ml) good-quality
honey

2 lbs (1 kg) apples (such
as Royal Gala, Pink Lady,
or Granny Smith), peeled
and chopped into 1-inch
(2.5 cm) dice

2 tsp pure vanilla extract

One day, my wife brought two of her friends, Tara and Kristen, into the kitchen at Crust to visit. As the curious beings they are, they inquired about ingredients and were enthralled by the inner workings of a commercial bakery. Taste-touring through the kitchen, we came across a combination of cooked caramel apples and vanilla bean. Upon giving it a taste, they beamed with delight at the subtle caramel and cooked fruit. Afterward, they texted my wife to say they couldn't stop thinking about it. They had deemed it irresistible and couldn't wait to taste it again. I dedicate this recipe to them.

1. Heat a large pot on medium-low heat for about 1 minute. Have the apple juice measured and ready nearby.

2. Sprinkle 3 tablespoons (37 g) of the sugar evenly over the bottom of the pot and carefully stir with a spatula until just dissolved. Sprinkle in another 3 tablespoons (37 g) of sugar and stir carefully until dissolved. Repeat until all the sugar has been added and has dissolved. The toffee should be a very pale golden color. Continue to stir carefully until it is a deep golden color, 2–6 minutes. The time depends greatly on your pot and your stove. The darker the color, the better the flavor will be, but don't let it burn. This can happen very quickly, so watch it carefully!

3. Use oven mitts for this step! There will be lots of steam and splatters, which can easily burn your skin. Extremely carefully and slowly, add the apple juice, a little at a time, stirring with a long-handled spoon between additions. When all the juice has been added, add the honey and bring the mixture to a boil. Cover and lower the heat to a simmer. Simmer gently for about 10 minutes or until the toffee has dissolved and the mixture is smooth.

4. Stir in the apples, cover, and cook for 20–30 minutes, stirring gently every 5 minutes, until the apples are opaque and tender when poked with a small sharp knife. Remove from the heat, stir in the vanilla, and let cool to room temperature.

5. Pour the apples and cooking liquid into an airtight container and refrigerate until ready to use.

These poached apples will keep in an airtight container in the fridge for up to 1 month. I don't recommend freezing them.

KITCHEN NOTE:

1. Once you've used the poached apples, the remaining liquid can be poured over ice cream.

Lemon or Raspberry Curd

MAKES ABOUT 2 CUPS (500 ML)

½ tsp powdered gelatin

1 Tbsp ice water

2 eggs, lightly whisked

½ cup (100 g) granulated sugar

1 Tbsp finely grated lemon zest, divided (for Lemon Curd only)

½ cup (125 ml) fresh lemon juice or raspberry juice (see notes)

⅔ cup (150 g) unsalted butter, at room temperature, cut into 1-inch (2.5 cm) cubes

---

KITCHEN NOTES:

1. Using freshly squeezed lemon or raspberry juice is imperative to the taste and texture of this curd. To make raspberry juice, place 2 cups (500 ml) thawed frozen raspberries in a sieve and push them with the back of a spoon or spatula to extract the juice. If you only have fresh raspberries, blitz them in a blender for a few seconds, then strain through a sieve.

2. Curd works best with acidic fruit, so while raspberries work great, strawberries, blackberries, and blueberries don't work quite as well. You can, however, get creative with citrus fruit, such as mandarin, grapefruit, or lime.

If you make lemon curd regularly, bravo! It belongs in all fridges and serves as an easy, light addition to any cake, cookie, or pie. Eating it by the spoonful is to be expected, standing with the fridge door open, maybe at midnight, maybe a little sneakily. With the bright lemony flavors prominent and the thick creaminess making it irresistible, this lemon curd is exceptional. Curd allows the fruit flavor to really shine, so give raspberries a try as well!

---

1. Place the gelatin in a small bowl and pour the ice water over it. Set aside while the water is absorbed, about 3 minutes.

2. Meanwhile, in a medium saucepan, whisk together the eggs and sugar. Whisk in half of the lemon zest (if making lemon curd) and the lemon or raspberry juice.

3. Place the saucepan over medium-low heat and bring to a simmer, whisking continuously. Lower the heat to low and continue to whisk for another 1–2 minutes or until the mixture has thickened. Don't let it boil.

4. Remove the pan from the heat and whisk in the gelatin. Continue to whisk for 1 minute to cool the curd slightly.

5. Pour the curd through a fine-mesh sieve into a large measuring jug. (Straining helps to remove any bits of undissolved gelatin or cooked egg.)

6. Using an immersion blender to help cool the curd, add the butter, one cube at a time, blending each completely before adding the next. (If you don't have an immersion blender, you can pour the curd into a stand blender and carefully blend on low speed with the lid on loosely so hot air escapes safely. You can also vigorously whisk in the butter by hand.)

7. If making lemon curd, add the remaining zest and blend well.

8. Let cool completely, then transfer to a glass jar with a tight-fitting lid. Refrigerate overnight before using.

This curd will keep in an airtight container in the fridge for up to 2 weeks. I don't recommend freezing it.

Dulce de Leche

1 can (300 ml) sweetened
condensed milk

½ tsp kosher salt

Dulce de leche sounds very fancy, but it's really not! It may taste like you've spent hours tending to dangerous molten caramel to obtain the exact right consistency, color, and flavor, but it's really just a humble can of sweetened condensed milk, left to cook and coax itself into a gorgeous, smooth, ribbony cascade of toffee-colored decadence.

1. Remove the label from the can of condensed milk and place the unopened can in a large pot of cold water. Make sure it is submerged in at least 2 inches (5 cm) of water. Cover the pot and bring to a boil over high heat.

2. Lower the heat to medium-low and simmer for 2½ hours, topping up the water as needed so that the can remains covered by 2 inches (5 cm) of water throughout.

3. Let the can cool in the water for at least 3 hours or overnight.

4. When completely cooled, open the can and scrape the dulce de leche into a mixing bowl. Add the salt and mix well.

This dulce de leche will keep in an airtight jar in the fridge for up to 1 month or in the freezer for up to 3 months. Thaw frozen dulce de leche overnight in the fridge before using.

Troubleshooting

Sometimes you follow a recipe to a tee and it still goes wrong. There is a lot of technique involved in baking, and that doesn't end with following the step-by-step process on the page. It includes how you prepare your baking pans, the age of your ingredients, and many other factors that can make or break a baked good. Here are some suggestions to fix a few of the more common baking problems, or at least explain why they may have happened. Take a deep breath, learn from your mistakes, and try again!

1. **Why won't my meringue rise/expand/whip/hold? It's loose and runny no matter how long I whip it.**

   ▸ Your equipment might have grease or moisture on it. Even the tiniest amount will prevent egg whites from whipping properly. Make sure your bowls, spoons, whisks, and hands are very clean and dry.

   ▸ Your egg whites might contain yolk. They must be completely free of yolk. To achieve this, crack the eggs into a small bowl, one by one, then transfer them to a larger bowl once you are sure each one is yolk-free.

2. **Why is my icing/frosting curdled and split? It just won't emulsify, no matter what I try.**

   ▸ Your butter might be too runny. It should be soft, but definitely not melted. Try popping the mixture in the fridge for a few minutes, then mixing again at high speed.

   ▸ Your butter might be too cold. Butter does not mix well if it is too stiff. Set the mixture aside until it comes to room temperature, then try mixing again on high speed.

3. **Why are my cookies melting into each other while they bake?**

   ▸ Your sheet pan might be too warm when you place the dough on it. Be sure to let the pan cool completely between batches and, if necessary, place it in the fridge for a few minutes.

   ▸ There might not be enough flour in the dough. My best tip? Weigh your flour to be sure your measurements are precise!

   ▸ Your oven might be too hot, causing the fat in the cookies to melt too fast. Double-check your oven temperature with a thermometer.

4. **Why does my cake have crusty, unappealing edges in some spots?**

   ▸ Your pan might not be greased evenly. Make sure it is, so the cake doesn't "fry" on one side.

5. **Why did my cakes come out burnt on the top/bottom and raw in the middle?**

   ▸ It might be too hot inside your oven.

- Check the temperature with a thermometer and adjust the oven as required. If you notice that your cake is burning before the baking time is up, loosely tent foil over it and continue baking.

- Your oven might have hot spots. You will learn where they are over time. If you know where your oven's hot spot is (mine is the back right corner), be sure to swap and/or rotate your cake pans as needed during baking.

- Make sure the rack is in the middle of the oven, so the cake is not too close to the burner. If you are baking multiple cakes on separate racks, swap their positions in the oven halfway through baking.

▸ You might be using thin, cheap cake pans. It is worth the investment to purchase heavy-duty pans!

▸ You might be using a cake pan that's the wrong size. If it's too deep, the center of the cake won't bake in the time allotted. If it's too shallow, the cake will require less baking time. Wherever possible, try to follow the recipe's recommended pan size.

6. **Why is my cake dense and gummy, not light and fluffy?**

▸ The butter and sugar might not be creamed together, either because the butter is too cold or because you haven't beaten it for long enough. If the recipe specifies that the mixture should be light and fluffy, be sure your butter is at room temperature, follow the recommended timing, and pay attention to the cues!

▸ You may have overmixed the batter. When mixing dry ingredients into wet ingredients, do so only until they are just combined.

7. **Why is my pastry falling apart when I mix it, and why does it crack when I roll it out?**

▸ It might be too dry. Gently mix in a touch of whatever liquid the recipe calls for.

▸ It might be too cold. Let it rest for a few minutes at room temperature, then try rolling it out again.

- You might have rolled it too fast. Be gentle with your pastry and roll it out slowly and mindfully.

8. **Why is my pastry not crispy and flaky?**

▸ Your dough might not be cold enough, which might melt its fat when you're mixing it with the flour. When the cold fat in the dough hits the hot oven, it melts slowly, creating steam and little pockets of air between the layers of pastry, which makes for a lovely flaky crust.

- It's best to mix with cool hands or use a pastry cutter or a fork.

- Be sure to chill the dough as recommended in the recipe.

▸ Your oven might not be hot enough.

- You might not have heated the oven long enough. When your oven beeps to tell you it's ready, leave it for another 15 minutes to be sure it reaches temperature.

- The oven door might have been open for too long when you put your pastry in. Place it quickly and close the oven door immediately! (This goes for all baking, by the way.)

9. **Why isn't my dough rising? The recipe says it should double or triple in size, and it doesn't seem to be budging.**

▸ Your dough may be too cold. Try putting it in a warmer spot, such as in the oven with the light on, or on a warm windowsill (not in direct sunlight). Once you figure out the warm spot in your kitchen that is best for proofing, you are golden.

▸ Your yeast may have expired. Check the expiry date and keep it fresh once opened by storing it in the fridge.

10. **Why is my chocolate seizing and/or separating when I try to melt it?**

‣ Your bowls, spoons, and whisks might not be clean and dry. Water is the enemy of chocolate when you are trying to melt it into a smooth, velvety consistency.

‣ You may have heated it at too high a temperature or left it on the heat for too long.

11. **Why are my brownies/muffins/loaves soggy on the bottom?**

‣ You might have left them to cool in the pan for too long. While it's sometimes best to let baked goods cool in the pan for a little while, if you leave them too long,

condensation will form and create a soggy bottom. Follow the recipe's recommendations and cool baked goods on a wire rack to allow air flow.

12. **Why do my baked goods always come out a little on the dry side?**

‣ Your measurements might be off. I've said it before, and I'll say it again: weigh your ingredients! Even 1–2 tablespoons of extra flour can dry out a cake or a cookie.

‣ You might be cutting into them too soon after taking them out of the oven. This releases steam and moisture, causing them to dry out. Let them cool as recommended.

"Thank Youz"

First, thank you to my beautiful wife, Pennye. "The way I see it . . ." Thank you for being my bright, shining beacon, for making me laugh, and for sharing my passion for food, cooking, and wonderful music. Your love and support are everything, and our kitchen dance parties are my favorite.

To Rebecca Wellman—thanks, Bex! From the first time we met, I knew we were two like-minded, passionate foodies who simply *had* to collaborate on a project like this. Your attention to detail, eye for perfection, and unwavering commitment to keeping me on task is truly amazing! Thank you for all your beautiful photographs, words, and inspiration. You are an incredible human.

Thanks to my fantastic four—Abby, Olivia, Sam, and Zac—for letting me take over the house with recipes, ingredients, and baked bits and pieces for over a year!

To those we couldn't have done this without: Emily Hodi, for being an absolute pastry rock star; Peter Bagi, for his fantastic talent and gorgeous contribution; Anna Olson, for such generous spirit and guidance; and Tanya Trafford, without whom we might not be where we are at all.

To my mum and dad, my brother Matt, and my sister, Jodie, for encouraging my love of cooking and baking from a very early age. And to my brother Si, I hope you pass the cooking torch on to your little one. Food is love in our family, and I love you all dearly.

Thank you to my business partner, Crystal, for the adventures we shared in a past life.

Special thanks to my kitchen manager, Sherin Pereira, for holding down the fort while I took on this project, and to all the Crust Bakery staff, past and present—thank you! Crust wouldn't be what it is today without you all. I am forever grateful.

Thank you to Rachel Brown, Whitney Millar, and Robert McCullough at Penguin Random House for the fantastic opportunity to create this book together, and to Jennifer Griffiths for her gorgeous design.

Finally, thank you to all our Crust customers from near and far, who, over the years, have made all those early mornings and gray hairs worth it. You are the reason we do this each and every day.

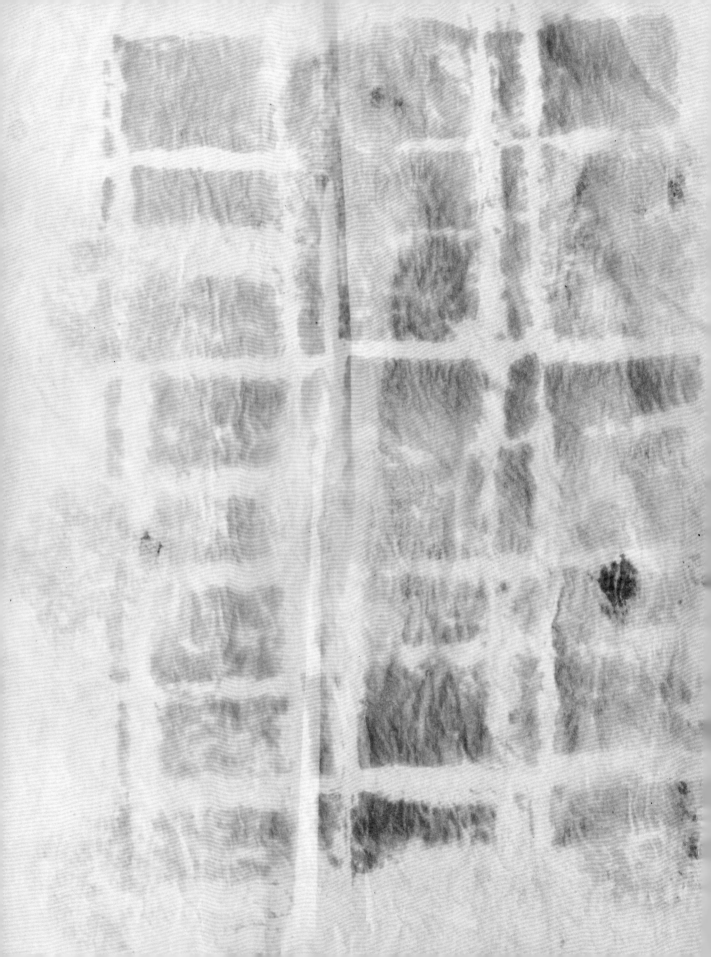

Index